Use of Computer

for BTEC level 2

Brian Perkes

HODDER AND STOUGHTON
LONDON SYDNEY AUCKLAND TORONTO

Brian Perkes B.Sc. Dip.O.R. is a Senior Analyst for ICI (Mond Division) and lectures at the North Cheshire College on mathematics, statistics and computing.

British Library Cataloguing in Publication Data

Perkes, Brian
   Use of computers for BTEC level 2.
   1. Engineering—Data processing
   I. Title
   001.64′02462   TA345

ISBN 0 340 33924 1

First printed 1984

Copyright © 1984 B.R.K. Perkes

All rights reserved. No part of this publication may be reproduced or transmitted in any form or by any means, electronic or mechanical, including photocopy, recording, or any information storage and retrieval system, without permission in writing from the publisher.

Typeset in 11/12pt Univers (monophoto) by Macmillan India Ltd, Bangalore

Printed in Great Britain for
Hodder and Stoughton Educational,
a division of Hodder and Stoughton Ltd.,
Mill Road, Dunton Green, Sevenoaks, Kent TN13 2YD,
by Robert Hartnoll Ltd, Bodmin, Cornwall

Contents

Preface ... iv

1 The Application of Computers ... 1

2 Computer Hardware ... 14

3 Computer Software ... 27

4 The BASIC Programming Language (I) ... 36

5 The BASIC Programming Language (II) ... 48

6 The BASIC Programming Language (III) ... 57

7 Program Flowcharts and Documentation ... 65

8 A Graph-Plotting Program ... 76

9 A Data-Retrieval Program ... 86

10 Systems Analysis ... 94

Appendix: Suggestions for Program Assignments ... 103

Index ... 107

Preface

This book is designed to cover the learning objectives of the two half units U80/719 and U80/720, 'Use of Computers' and 'Computer Assignments', at level II of the Business and Technician Education Council. It aims to introduce the uses, principles and applications of computers, to foster skills in the high-level BASIC programming language, and to enable the student to gain an awareness through practice of the uses to which computers can be put.

The early chapters deal with the computer and its industrial environment. The BASIC language is then introduced and illustrated with many practical examples. Two detailed program explanations each form the basis for chapters to bring out good programming practices, and provide frameworks for the student to build on. Systems analysis and documentation topics are also covered, to help the student to manage his own assignments as well as to provide a perspective on these activities in the general application of computers.

I would like to thank my wife and children for not complaining too much during the writing of the book, and also to acknowledge the help given by ICI plc (Mond Division) and Nalfloc Ltd in supplying the specially commissioned photographs of computer installations. A final, special word of thanks is due to Maurice Haslehurst, former Dean of the Faculty of Technology and Science, North Cheshire College, who, from his experience as author of companion volumes of Manufacturing Technology textbooks, provided invaluable guidance in the early stages of this book's development.

B.R.K.P.
Comberbach 1983

1 The Application of Computers

1.1 Types of computer

If we have some information, in the form of numbers or text, and a set of rules which we can apply to the information to produce some desired result, then a computer could be used to carry out the process for us. What distinguishes a computer from less sophisticated devices is the flexibility it gives us to specify what the rules are. This book describes the use of digital computers (the sort that produce our electricity bills, payslips and road-tax reminders amongst other useful things). Digital computers obtain their results by performing arithmetic processes (such as addition or multiplication) on the original data. The rules we specify to carry out the processing are defined in special lines of text which together make up a computer program.

The other type of computer, which we shall not discuss in detail because its applications are limited to a special class of problem, is known as the analogue computer. Analogue computers make use of the physical characteristics of one system (e.g. an electric current passing through a circuit with resistors and capacitors) to model, or provide an analogue to, the behaviour of some other system (e.g. the response of a car's suspension system to a bumpy road).

To change the rules for an analogue computer, using resistors and capacitors for example, it is necessary to change physically the configuration of these items in the circuit. Analogue computers are used where the mathematical solution of a problem would be so complex and tortuous that it is more efficient in terms of setting up and processing the problem to use analogue, rather than digital, methods. Typically this occurs when complicated mathematical equations are required, as is the case when analysing reactions within an industrial chemical process, flight characteristics of aircraft, or responses in vehicle suspension systems. Hybrid computers combine analogue and digital functions but are even more specialised than analogue machines.

1.2 Types of digital computer

There are three recognised categories of digital computer: the mainframe computer, the minicomputer and the microcomputer. In broad terms these categories can be related to physical size, a mainframe occupying a large room, a mini requiring only a small room and a micro sitting on a desk-top. Similarly, we may relate their size to what the computers can do. We find that mainframes support many different applications at the same time with several telecommunications links to remote locations. Minis support a limited number of applications at the same time with one or two telecommunications links. Micros support one application at a time, perhaps with more than one user sharing access to the computer at the same time.

The distinction between the categories has been blurred however by the continuing development of the microprocessor. A microprocessor uses the technology of the silicon chip, a wafer of material a few millimetres square which can out-perform a cabinet full of transistorised circuit boards. In the early stages of their development microprocessors were limited to controlling very small computers, so that microprocessors and microcomputers came to mean the same thing to many people. As computer manufacturers develop the full potential of microprocessors, however, they will be no longer limited to microcomputers, and categorisation should be by what the computer does rather than by how it works, although as machines become more powerful even this distinction is dubious.

1.3 Types of digital computing

Before discussing several examples of computing applications (see Section 1.4) it is worth considering the broad categories into which these fall. In each example it is the computer's ability to do the arithmetic (including picking out all the items that belong to a certain group) very much faster than is humanly possible, that justifies its cost. This applies either where a lot of similar calculations need to be repeated or where a single relatively complex calculation is required. The point of using computers can be either to reduce human involvement in a situation (perhaps to reduce wage bills or maybe to reduce risk in hazardous environments) or to achieve a quality of information that would not be attainable any other way.

(i) Scientific/technical applications. These cover the use of computers in research environments for pure and applied sciences, for industrial engineering design and for the management sciences including economics and operational research. The

essence of this type of application is a mathematical relationship which requires a lot of calculation. The colloquial term for this type of investigation is 'number crunching'.

(ii) Real-time applications. These are uses where it is important to have an immediate response from a computer, based on information which may change rapidly but which is currently up-to-date. Systems to be used for airline or hotel bookings, credit-card control or process control in industry are all in this category. An information retrieval system which, for example, displayed titles of books held in a library, but which only updated the information once a month, would not be considered a real-time application.

(iii) Commercial data-processing applications. These have always been the traditional bread and butter customers for the computer manufacturers, and are made up of accountancy, payroll, salary, stock-control, sales order, invoice and similar systems which would have had their quill-pen equivalents in a business during the time of Charles Dickens. Typically these applications require little by way of calculation, but use the computer's high speed to process large volumes of transactions very quickly.

(iv) Recreational applications. Relatively recently the advent of the microprocessor has led to powerful microcomputers being sold for a few hundred pounds. This change in computer prices has led to the growth of a hobby market in which arcade-type games, fantasy adventure games and even computer art can be enjoyed.

Finally in this section it is appropriate to give a very short glossary of terms used to describe the methods of processing which may be adopted to implement a particular application.

Batch processing. Originally the only form of processing, this involves all the relevant data for a particular task (e.g. hours worked, payment rates and employee details for a payroll system) being fed in to the computer over a relatively short period of time, so that processing can take place and the results be produced almost immediately. Typically a batch process may require several files of different types of data to be sorted into sequence for processing.

Distributed processing. This is the term given to configurations where the input/output devices to the main computer are themselves effectively microcomputers, so that a lot of the processing is done either before the input data is sent to the main machine (e.g. preliminary calculations or checking) or on output data sent from the main machine, before the output is displayed. The advantage of this type of configuration is that it takes some of the load off the main computer, allowing it to concentrate on those things which it does most efficiently.

Interactive computing or time-sharing. This type of processing allows an individual to input some data at any time that is convenient. The use of the computer is effectively shared between a number of users but the appearance to each of them is of almost immediate response from the machine. If the machine needs to read any of the data stores to which it is linked then this will be done, and an answer or response produced so that a dialogue or interaction takes place between the users and the computer.

Multi-task processing This form of processing is employed by most large mainframes (and some smaller machines) and allows the computer to get on with more than one job at once—for example batch processing and interactive computing. The objective of this complication is to make the best use of all the computer's facilities, so that if for example one job requires a lot of 'number crunching' while another job makes heavy demands on input or output devices, then both may run simultaneously and finish in a shorter elapsed time than would otherwise be required.

Off-line processing. This is batch processing where a vital file of information (e.g. employee details) is not usually available to the computer, so that even if one file of data is available (e.g. the hours worked by each employee) then processing (for example the payroll calculation) cannot take place immediately.

On-line processing. This is batch or interactive processing where a relevant file of data is permanently available to the system, or on-line, so that processing can take place whenever the user wishes. An example would be the customer-details file for an on-line system handling sales orders.

The glossary should enable the reader to decipher expressions like 'real-time on-line batch processing' (see Section 1.4(c) for an example) but it should not encourage the proliferation of such expressions!

1.4 Some case studies

(a) A commercial mainframe

Consider a large manufacturing business with, say, in excess of 10 000 employees and a large mainframe computer for its commercial data-processing applications. Because the computer will have cost several millions of pounds it is an asset that must be made to earn its keep, and it will be operated twenty-four hours a day on a shift basis. Many different applications will be operated on the machine. Each application will typically consist of a large number of programs and data files and will be referred to as a system. Very often the files from one system may also play a part in another system. For example the payroll system which will calculate the wages of the weekly-paid staff will use a file of data containing employee details, and a file of data containing hours worked by individuals to produce another file of data giving the wages to be paid. Now the employee details file may well be part of a personnel system used to analyse such things as the age distribution of employees or the number of qualified tradesmen. Similarly the file of wages to be paid will certainly have to play a part in the company's accountancy system. For a large firm such as this the accounts system itself will be very sophisticated, involving the weekly collection of data from administrative and manufacturing centres, so that on a monthly basis financial

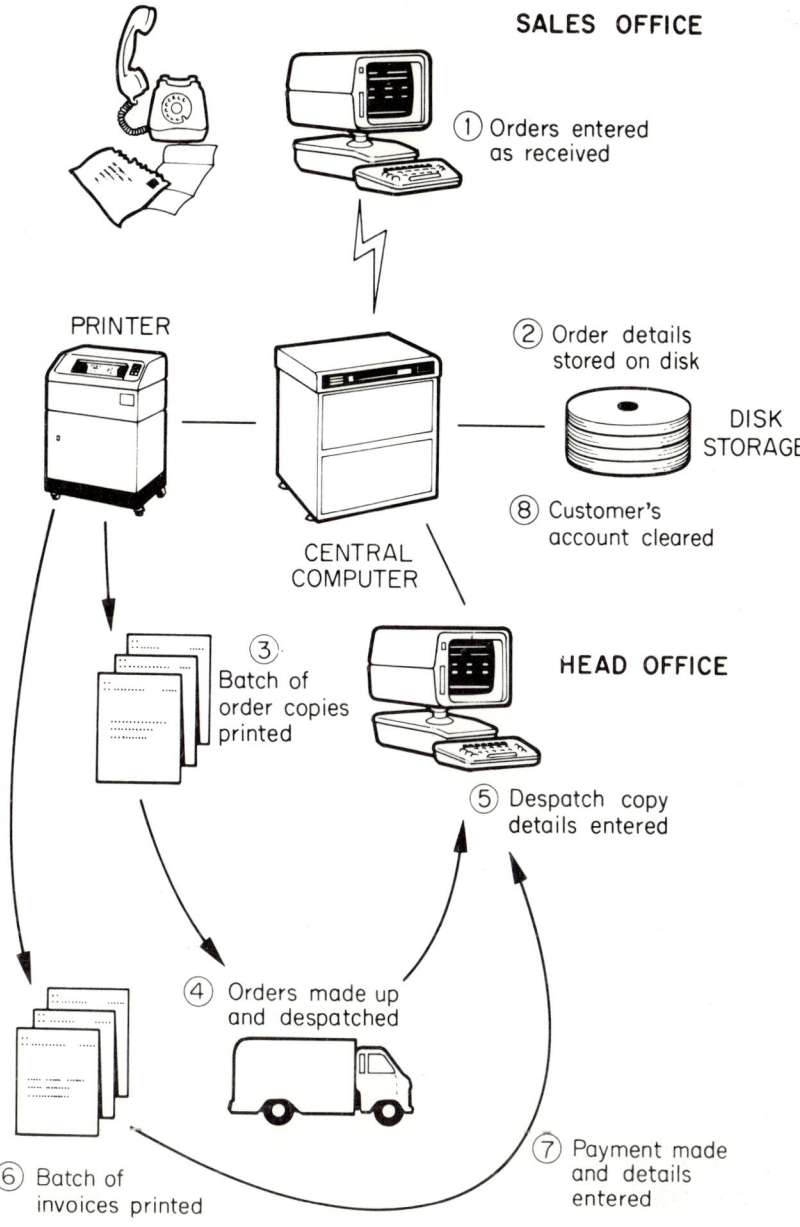

Fig. 1.1 A simplified order/invoice system. Modelled on the ICL System 25.

performances and targets can be compared. It is possible that on-line interrogation facilities may be available so that the current position can be seen as required.

Customer orders will be entered directly into the computer from the sales departments and the necessary despatch notes, delivery notes and invoices will be produced (see Figure 1.1). It is likely that such a large firm will have several sales offices scattered around the country, and that these will have telecommunications links with the central computer, so that data entered at keyboards at the remote sites is input directly to the computer. Despatch and delivery notes may also be printed out at remote works or depot sites by means of similar links. Checks on the credit-worthiness of customers will be an automatic feature of the system. It is worth mentioning here the steps required to reduce the number of errors. For example it is possible for the computer to check that the product ordered by a particular customer has been purchased before by him (giving the sales clerk a warning if not) and it is also possible to check the quantity (upper and lower limits being set to avoid obviously silly deliveries). Validity checking of this sort is important since mistakes in data input are the chief cause of computer errors. Insufficiently tested programs are the other main cause, machine failures being insignificant by comparison. An office using such a commercial mainframe computer is shown in Figure 1.2.

Fig. 1.2 An office with terminals connected to a commercial mainframe computer.

Another function which the computer will be used for will be the purchasing, supply, and stock-control system. This will hold details of all purchase orders issued by the company (so that progress and outstanding items can be monitored—probably on-line) and will record the stock levels in all the company's local supply stores, giving automatic warnings when replenishment should be put in hand.

In the midst of our awe at the technological wizardry of computers we should never lose sight of the fact that computer applications need people to design and operate them. Computer operators attending to a large mainframe installation are shown in Figure 1.3. The term 'liveware' is sometimes used to refer to these support staff, and large installations like the one in our example employ them in the following main categories:

computer operators   to control the machine and its peripheral devices, loading data on tapes or disks, and changing printer paper etc.;

applications programmers   to write programs for the computer applications;

Fig. 1.3 Computer operators working on a large mainframe installation.

systems programmers to write programs to control and monitor the way in which the computer performs its tasks;

systems analysts to design ways of applying computer programs to business procedures (specifying what the programs should do).

(b) A scientific/technical mainframe

If the manufacturing firm in the last example had centralised research and development departments, engineering design departments, and employed management science techniques, then it may well have a second mainframe dedicated to these functions. The performance of a distillation column for example, used to separate chemicals, may depend on the type of packing material used in the column, the height of the column, the temperature of the material at the inlet point etc., and a mathematical relationship will be known by the design engineer. A computer program can be used to compare the costs and performances of several possible designs and so enable the best to be chosen.

Very often a business situation will involve random factors which although understood cannot be readily handled mathematically. Examples of this are chemical processes involving intermediate stock tanks with plant items liable to breakdown, or customers queueing at supermarket checkouts. In this type of situation, simulation can be a useful technique. Simulation involves using the computer to generate the sequences of random events (like customer arrivals) and also to calculate the effects on the system from one event to the next. In this way the effects of certain sizes of stock tank or a certain number of checkouts can be examined for a vast number of different random sequences, and an estimate of the best configuration obtained. Simulation makes use of the computer's ability to perform repetitive calculations quickly, to achieve what would be impracticable using human efforts alone.

There are many techniques which make use of the computer's untiring calculating power to solve technical problems. An important class of technique draws on the field of the analysis of numbers and obtains the required answer by a repetitive or iterative process. In this technique a first guess solution is refined to produce a better guess which is then itself refined and so on until the answer is acceptably accurate. When such techniques are used for modelling business situations however it is important to remember that the quality of the answer is only as good as the extent to which the mathematical representation models reality.

(c) A commercial minicomputer

A medium sized manufacturing business with a few hundred employees, purchasing a computer for the first time, may well choose a minicomputer costing a few tens of thousands of pounds. The applications it will be used for will almost certainly include the payroll and accounts applications mentioned for the commercial mainframe. However one important difference is that the programs used for these applications will probably have been purchased 'off the shelf' as applications packages sold by firms specialising in this kind of software (software is the term used to describe computer programs as distinct from the machinery, or hardware). Also, because the machine represents a smaller capital investment than a commercial mainframe computer, it may only be used during working hours and have only one or two people with a part-time responsibility for looking after its operation. Figures 1.4 and 1.5 show the machine room for a minicomputer installation and the office terminals.

Such a machine would be capable of handling the order/invoicing type of system discussed for the mainframe, but in a more limited way with a smaller volume of transactions. Order data would be entered from keyboards in offices near to the computer, and the documents would be produced on a single

Fig. 1.4 The machine room for a minicomputer.

Fig. 1.5 An office with a terminal connected to a commercial minicomputer.

printer next to the computer. So as not to interfere with the printing taking place for accounts applications, for example, the printing of despatch notes or invoices would be done in batches. Order information may be built up on-line in real time (as orders are telephoned in) to be batch processed at set times during the day, ready for delivery by hand to the works. Similarly, details of goods despatched will be supplied by the works to be put in to the computer and matched with the order file so that a batch of invoices can be produced to catch the post.

(d) A small business microcomputer

Microcomputers costing a few hundred to a few thousand pounds are found in departments of large firms and as the only computer in small businesses. Figure 1.6 shows one being used. Without data storage facilities they can be useful to calculate the cost of such diverse things as, for example, kitchen designs or yachts which may be tailored to the needs of the potential customer, printing out a record of the specification and the price.

The Application of Computers 11

Fig. 1.6 A microcomputer for small businesses or scientific applications.

With data storage facilities (naturally of smaller capacity than those of larger machines) the range of potential applications is virtually limitless but can be categorised into two broad types.

(i) File display and search. Here the microcomputer is used to enable a file of records to be created and maintained. Examples might include details of:
    houses for sale by an estate agent;
    delivery vehicles and their service history;
    training records of employees;
    equipment location, manufacturer, and reliability;
    customer names, addresses, and goods purchased.
Depending on the amount of data to be held for each item a few hundred to several thousand records could be handled. The data from any one record could be displayed on request, and more importantly, because of the saving in clerical effort that it represents, it is possible to have the computer search through all the data listing records that match on some specified criteria. For example:

all houses in a particular price range and in a particular district;
all vehicles due for a regular service in the next month;
all employees who have not attended a safety course;
all electrical equipment from a certain manufacturer;
all customers who bought a carpet five years ago.

(ii) File accumulation and summary. Here we are involved with book keeping and accountancy systems. These can range from details of sales and purchases (kept to control stocks and produce regular sales-volume and financial-performance summaries) to payroll systems. This type of application requires that the data produced should be reliable, and for this reason the design of such systems must be given the same sort of care and attention as their mainframe counterparts.

1.5 The office of the future

Many businesses now use word processors. These machines consist of a keyboard, a visual display screen, a printer and some type of computer storage device. Currently these are dedicated to the task of setting up and editing large volumes of text, achieving much higher efficiencies than are possible using traditional typing methods. Some of these machines are virtually specialised stand-alone microcomputers and require no links with any other computer. The benefits of having a word-processing unit linked to a business computer are however being discovered, and are leading to a convergence of computing, word processing and telecommunications.

Current technology has led to many installations having a configuration which has attracted the title of 'The Office of the Future'. A group of managers and secretaries is equipped with its own keyboards and visual-display-screen workstations. Each workstation contains sufficient microprocessor hardware to operate as a stand-alone word processor, but it is also capable of being easily linked to any computers the business operates. The result is a system which allows 'documents' to be displayed on any desired screen, enabling the preparation and passing of documents between managers and secretaries to take place even more efficiently. It also enables messages to be sent, files of information to be retrieved and any technical programs to be accessed and used, all without the manager having to leave his desk. It is to be hoped that this step forward leads to lean, efficient businesses and not fat, lazy managers!

Exercises 1

1 Think of a computer system which you or your family have been associated with. What files of data do you think it requires in order to operate?
2 Specify some validity checks for data input to any real or imaginary computer system. These checks show when any obviously silly information has been keyed in.
3 Think of a business of any kind, or educational establishment that you are familiar with. In what ways could it benefit from the use of a computer?
4 Think of a mathematical problem that a computer could help you to solve. Explain the steps that the computer would have to cope with.
5 Think of a game that you would like to play on a computer. What aspects of the game might be difficult to set up and why?

2 Computer Hardware

2.1 The structure of a computer

The construction of the machinery or hardware of early computers involved a few units whose functions were clear-cut and easy to define. The development of more sophisticated internal architectures, and the advent of microprocessors in particular, have made it more difficult to give an accurate general description of computer structure. However, with the aid of Figure 2.1 we

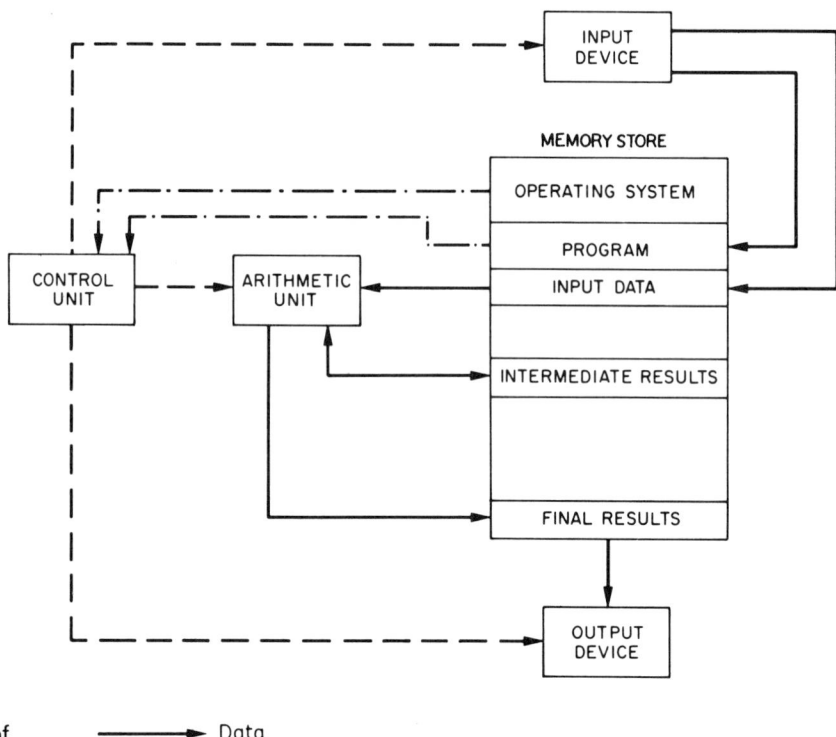

Fig. 2.1 The concepts of computer structure and operation.

⟶ Data
--- ⟶ Control commands
—·— ⟶ Coded instructions

can discuss the underlying concepts of both structure and operation. We will start by considering each of the five units that are shown in the diagram.

Input devices. As their name suggests input devices allow information to be communicated to the computer. Simple examples are a punched-card reader, a paper-tape reader and a games paddle as used for many video-games. The distinctive feature of these devices is that they communicate one way only, from the user to the computer, so that an output device is required for the computer to communicate the results of its deliberations. Some devices combine input and output functions. Magnetic-tape drives and magnetic-disk drives are good examples, and a visual display unit with keyboard input facility falls into this category. Section 2.3 gives full details of these devices.

Output devices. The most common simple output device is a printer, communicating results from the computer to the user via the printed page (the term 'hardcopy' is used to distinguish this kind of output from that of transient screen displays). Card punches, paper-tape punches and even sound amplifiers can be one way computer-output devices.

Memory store. The memory store can be thought of as a set of pigeon holes each with its own reference address, in which data or instructions can be stored. Physically the mechanisms for achieving this storage have changed as technology has advanced. The essential point is that this memory is the working memory of the computer, as opposed to data stored in the media of any peripheral device such as a magnetic-disk drive or tape drive. Speed of access to this memory plays a fundamental part in determining the performance of the computer. Historically the cost of providing this memory was a limiting factor on computer performance, and a less expensive but slower backing store was used in conjunction with it to achieve the desired results economically. Microprocessor technology has largely overcome the cost limitation but is currently grappling with the technical problems of co-ordinating many individual 'chips', or engineering ever larger and more sophisticated versions. In the context of microprocessor storage the following two terms need explanation.

ROM stands for read only memory and refers to a form of memory which is pre-programmed with fixed information that can be read by the computer but cannot be modified without very special equipment.

RAM stands for random access memory. This is the portion of memory in a microcomputer which is under the control of the user and which he may direct the computer to write information to, or to read information from.

Arithmetic unit. The arithmetic unit is that part of the hardware which performs the arithmetic calculations (such as addition or multiplication) and logical comparisons required by the computer program. It is important to realise that all calculations and comparisons are broken down to simple operations involving strings of the binary digits 0 and 1.

Control unit. The control unit is the hardware that receives instructions, interprets them into actions for the other units, and initiates those actions.

2.2 Operations involving the five units

In order to function the computer requires a fundamental set of rules to guide the operation of the control unit which exercises overall control over the computer system and supervises the running of other programs. These rules are described as the 'operating system' of the machine and will be held in the memory store. The operating system can either be read into memory via a fast input device such as a magnetic-disk drive, or it can be held permanently available to the machine as in a ROM chip for example. In the latter case the concept of firmly-fixed operating software has given rise to the term 'firmware'.

On start-up of the computer, the operating system will be made available automatically to the memory store, and the machine will

Fig. 2.2 At the controls of a large mainframe installation.

await further instructions or commands via an input device, such as a visual display unit. Typically this command will ask the machine to read in or load a certain program from a certain input device, and this will result in the program (which we remember is itself a set of instructions) residing in the memory store. Upon a further command to run or execute this program, the control unit will examine in sequence the individual instructions of the program, and initiate actions appropriately. For example the first requirement of the program may be to read in several items of data from an input device.

The control unit will initiate data input and assign the data to specified locations in the memory store. Subsequently some calculations may be required involving these data, and for this purpose the control unit will call on the functions of the arithmetic unit, transferring the immediate results back to the memory store in new locations. This process may be repeated to produce final results in the memory store, and upon the control unit interpreting an instruction from the program to feed out the results, they will be displayed on whatever device has been specified. Figure 2.2 shows a large mainframe computer being used.

The flow lines in Figure 2.1 illustrate the activities described above. In particular it is worth noting that when the program is first read into the memory it is effectively as a flow of data. The lines of program text do not become instructions until they are interpreted as such by the control unit, which also follows the instructions of the operating system, and issues its control commands to the arithmetic unit and input and output devices. The process of program interpretation as described above is in fact a simplification but further discussion of it is best left to Chapter 3.

2.3 Details of input and output devices

(a) Magnetic-disk drives

Let us start our consideration of this type of device with the floppy disks (Figure 2.3) used in desk-top microcomputers and some word-processing machines. These are disks of some 12.7 cm (the mini-floppy disk) or 19.7 cm (the larger-floppy disk) diameter, made of a rather flimsy-looking plastic material that flops easily and has a surface coating of a magnetic medium. They are permanently encased in a square cardboard envelope which allows them to be handled without damaging the magnetic surface, and which makes them rigid enough to be inserted in the slots of the disk drives. The disk drives spin the disks in much the same way as a record on a turntable, with the important

18 Use of Computers

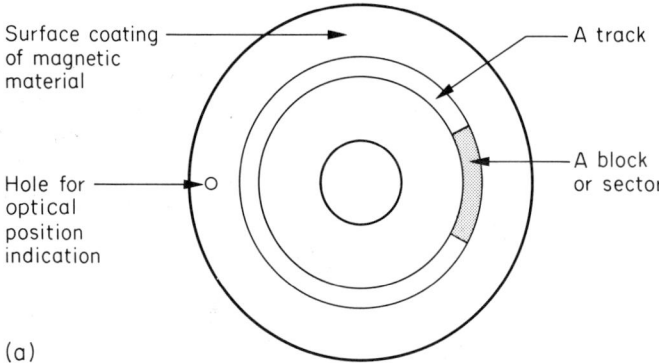

(a)

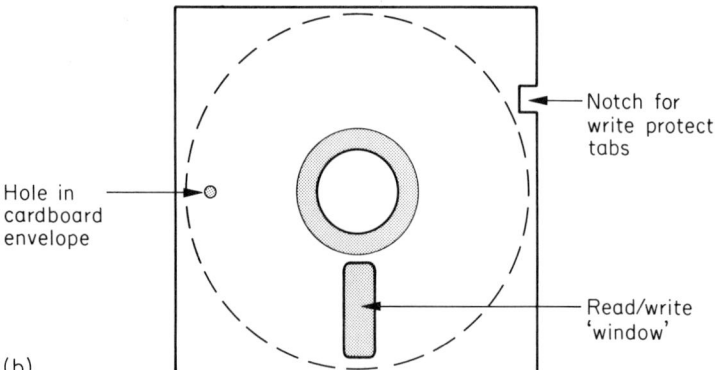

(b)

Fig. 2.3 The floppy disk. (a) The disk. (b) The cardboard envelope.

difference that the information is stored in concentric tracks which can be read from or written to by a single read/write head which can vary its radial distance from the centre of the disk. Typically a floppy disk may have about 40 tracks each capable of storing about 2500 characters, giving it a total capacity of some 100 000 characters. Since a full A4 page of typescript represents about 2000 characters, this represents a capacity of about 50 such pages. The suffix K is often used loosely to represent the quantity 1000 in computer literature,* so that the disk capacity above would be described as 100K characters or bytes, the unit of storage commonly required to represent a character in binary notation. The term double density is employed for systems in which the same size disk is used to hold information in about 80 tracks. Normally only one side of a floppy disk is used. Each track is split up into some ten or so blocks or sectors, each of which is identified to the disk drive by its position on the track relative to a special marker hole on the disk which enables optical sensors to control the rotational position of the disk read or write operations.

* In computer terminology $1 K = 2^{10} = 1024$

The cardboard envelope has a window to allow data transfer between the magnetic medium and the read/write head, and a notch which has the function of allowing writing to take place when it is uncovered, but which inhibits writing (by means of optical sensing) when the notch is covered by purpose-made

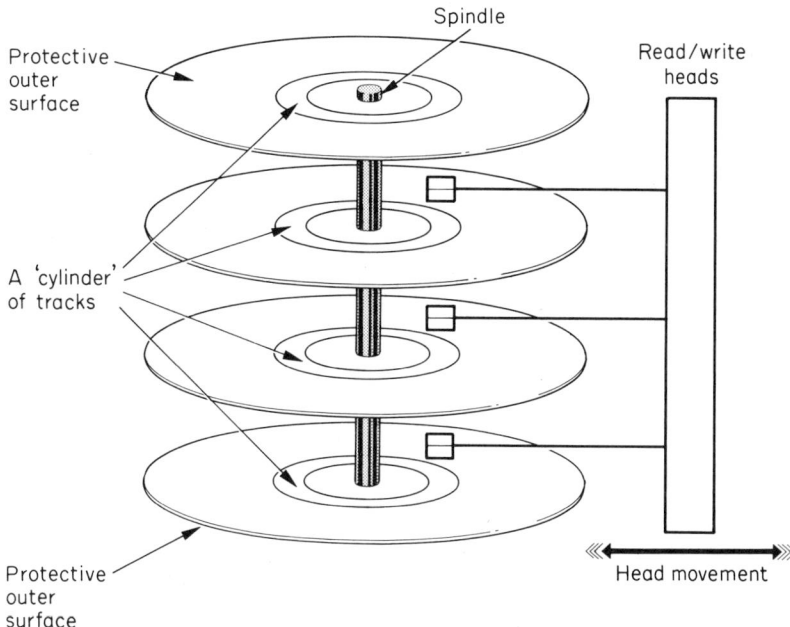

Fig. 2.4 A pack of hard disks.

sticky tabs. This is a protection device to avoid accidental corruption of important data.

Moving on to the so-called hard disks (Figure 2.4) we have packs of several rigid disks with a common axis, the interior disks being coated with magnetic material and being read from or written to by a comb of read/write heads. The same concepts of tracks and sectors apply here with the additional term 'cylinder' used to describe a set of tracks positioned vertically above each other, the information from each of which can be read without requiring movement of the comb of read/write heads. The capacities of this type of disk vary and are measured in terms of millions of bytes or megabytes (MB), typically they may range from 16 MB for a small minicomputer to several hundred MB for a large mainframe. The disk packs described here are loaded onto a disk drive to be used, but a separate class of disks, known as Winchester technology disks, have their own integral disk drive and are sealed units. These are a relatively cheap way of achieving large storage capacities for micro and minicomputers. The key factors in disk device speed are:

(i) seek time—the average time taken for the read/write heads to move to the cylinder position required;

(ii) latency time—the average time taken for the required sector to become positioned over the read/write heads;
(iii) transfer time—the time taken to transfer a sector of data once correctly positioned.

Total access time for a particular block will be of the order of 20 to 100 milliseconds (thousandths of a second), but when blocks are processed sequentially transfer rates of the order of 100 000 characters per second are feasible. A bank of large hard-disk drives is shown in Figure 2.5.

Fig. 2.5 A bank of large hard-disk drives.

Advantages of disk devices. The ability of a read/write head to move directly to the track containing the required block of data, as opposed to having to perform laborious sequential reading of all preceding data, is this device's main advantage. The terms direct access or random access are used to describe this type of process, and it leads to very speedy retrieval of stored data. Floppy disks and disk packs also require a minimum of handling effort, unlike magnetic tapes for example, which always have rewinding needs and can require initial threading. Disks can

Computer Hardware 21

also have considerably greater storage capacity than magnetic tapes.

Disadvantages of disk devices. The main disadvantage of disk devices is that they are a relatively expensive form of storage. This is mainly due to the technical sophistication of their construction, which also makes them liable to data corruption and mechanical faults. Disks also require a certain degree of delicacy when handled, unlike the relatively robust magnetic tapes.

(b) Magnetic-tape drives

These devices function in a way similar to that of domestic audio tape recorders, with a read/write head having tape coated with a magnetic medium fed across it. Microcomputers generally employ cassette drives, whilst larger machines operate with higher capacity and higher speed reels. As with disks, data are stored in blocks of perhaps several hundred characters (on some systems this blocksize is variable to optimise operations). However the key difference between tape and disk based data files is that the tape files must be accessed sequentially. For example if we have an alphabetically sorted file of customers names, addresses and credit ratings etc. and we wish to find the details of a customer called Smith, then it will be necessary to read through all the preceeding customers' details before the

Fig. 2.6 A magnetic-tape drive being used.

required information is found. The attraction of direct access on a disk is obvious but nonetheless economic considerations make magnetic tape storage a sensible choice for situations where a significant amount of data has to be stored cheaply, and where sequential processing is practical (such as processing a payroll for example). It should be noted that because of the sequential nature of tape operations it is normal to update files by reading the original together with a file of updates, and writing out a completely new file of both unchanged and updated records. As a guide to tape capacities, a recording density of about 200 characters per cm with a tape speed of 200 cm per second enables a rate of transfer of some 40 000 characters per second to be achieved. A full reel containing blocks of 400 characters each would at this density give a total tape capacity of nearly eight megabytes. Figure 2.6 shows a magnetic-tape drive being used.

Advantages of magnetic-tape devices. Magnetic tape devices provide a relatively cheap and robust way of storing and retrieving data.

Disadvantages of magnetic-tape devices. Sequential processing can be a very slow operation (rewinding requirements add to this) and can require a significant number of tape-drive devices to handle each separate file. Operator intervention is relatively high for magnetic tapes because of the need to load each file separately. Storage capacities are not in general as high as for disk drives, and a disk drive processing sequentially can achieve faster rates of data transfer.

(c) Visual display units

Visual display units (VDUs) comprise a television-type screen with either an integral or loosely attached typewriter-like keyboard. They provide an on-line way of interacting with a computer and can be used to create/edit a program or to control the execution of a program, accepting data input from the keyboard (perhaps displaying the input) and displaying the output results. Because of the limitations of their human operators they are not ideal for the initial capture of very large quantities of data, but are well suited to interrogation applications and program editing.

Advantages of VDUs. VDUs are relatively cheap devices which can be widely distributed to allow a large number of people to have on-line interaction with a computer, being especially suited to interrogation-type applications with small amounts of data input.

Disadvantages of VDUs. They are not suited to the input or output of large quantities of data. If large numbers of VDU devices are attached to a computer system then they can impose a significant overhead on the computer's housekeeping resources (sharing time between devices and controlling them)

Computer Hardware 23

and severely degrade its performance.

(d) Serial printers

Serial printers produce computer output one character at a time, with speeds of the order of 30–120 characters per second (with considerable variation betweeen manufacturers and type of machine). They are suitable for creating a permanent record of relatively small quantities of data, and may be used in conjunction with a VDU, printing only selected results for example. The mechanisms used to achieve the impression include golf-ball like print heads which are hammered against the page when suitably orientated, matrix print heads which hammer a selection of small matrix elements against the page to represent characters (or where ink ribbons are not used, employ heat-sensitive or electrically-sensitive papers to record the matrix elements) and daisy-wheel printers which spin a many-petalled vertical print wheel so that the required character can be hammered onto the page.

Fig. 2.7 An IBM laser printer.

Advantages of serial printers. These are the cheapest devices for producing hard-copy output. Daisy-wheel printers are at the top end of the price range but produce good correspondence-quality print.

Disadvantages of serial printers. Their speeds are too low for the output of very large volumes of data. Their advantage of local availability is tempered by the fact that they can be very noisy, although this can be reduced by appropriate shielding.

(e) Line printers

The serial, character by character, manner of operation of the devices described above seriously limits the overall speed of printing. By contrast, line printers are designed to print a whole line in one operation and can achieve speeds that are hard to comprehend, 300 to 2000 lines per minute being a representative range. Chain printers are the most common, the principle involving a chain of type characters driven continuously at high speed, print hammers being synchronised to strike the paper and ink ribbon against the moving type under precise control. Ink-jet and laser are emerging printer technologies, currently at the very high quality, high price end of the market. A laser printer is shown in Figure 2.7.

Advantages of line printers. High speeds make these devices ideal for applications involving a high volume of throughput.

Disadvantages of line printers. These devices are expensive and not portable, and generally produce a relatively poor print quality.

(f) Paper-tape readers, card readers and key-to-disk systems

These devices represent both ends of the technology spectrum, paper-tape and card readers and punches being much in evidence in earlier generations of computer systems, with key-to-disk systems being much more commonly used today. The method of recognising data for paper tape and card relied on holes punched through them in coded form being interpreted by optical or electrical sensors in their respective readers. Although relative simplicity brought them a mass market they were always unpopular as a medium with users and operators alike because of their flimsiness and, in the case of cards, added vulnerability to shuffling. These days, where a need for large scale data preparation is required, a key-to-disk system will often be employed. This consists of keyboard data-entry stations with small, local, floppy-disk storage which can be transferred directly to on-line hard-disk units when the data has been verified. Typical speeds for fast paper-tape readers were 1000 characters per second, and for card readers 1000 cards (containing up to 80 characters each) per minute. These speeds, although apparently fast, are very slow compared to magnetic-tape and disk devices, and this slowness has contributed to their demise.

Advantages. Paper tape and card devices are relatively unsophisticated and hence relatively cheap. The medium, although flimsy, is at least robust to handling with dirty fingers! Key-to-disk systems are the speediest and most efficient way of feeding large amounts of data to a computer, particularly since modern computers would find slower input devices caused severe bottlenecks.

Disadvantages. Slow processing and operating problems due to tearing are the main disadvantages of card and paper-tape readers, whilst key-to-disk systems have no serious disadvantages apart from their high cost.

(g) Sensing and controlling devices

A discussion of input/output devices would not be complete without mention of devices which sense conditions, relay them to a computer and initiate appropriate action. For example, a chemical plant effluent may be fundamentally acidic and require neutralisation with an alkali (see Figure 2.8). A computerised

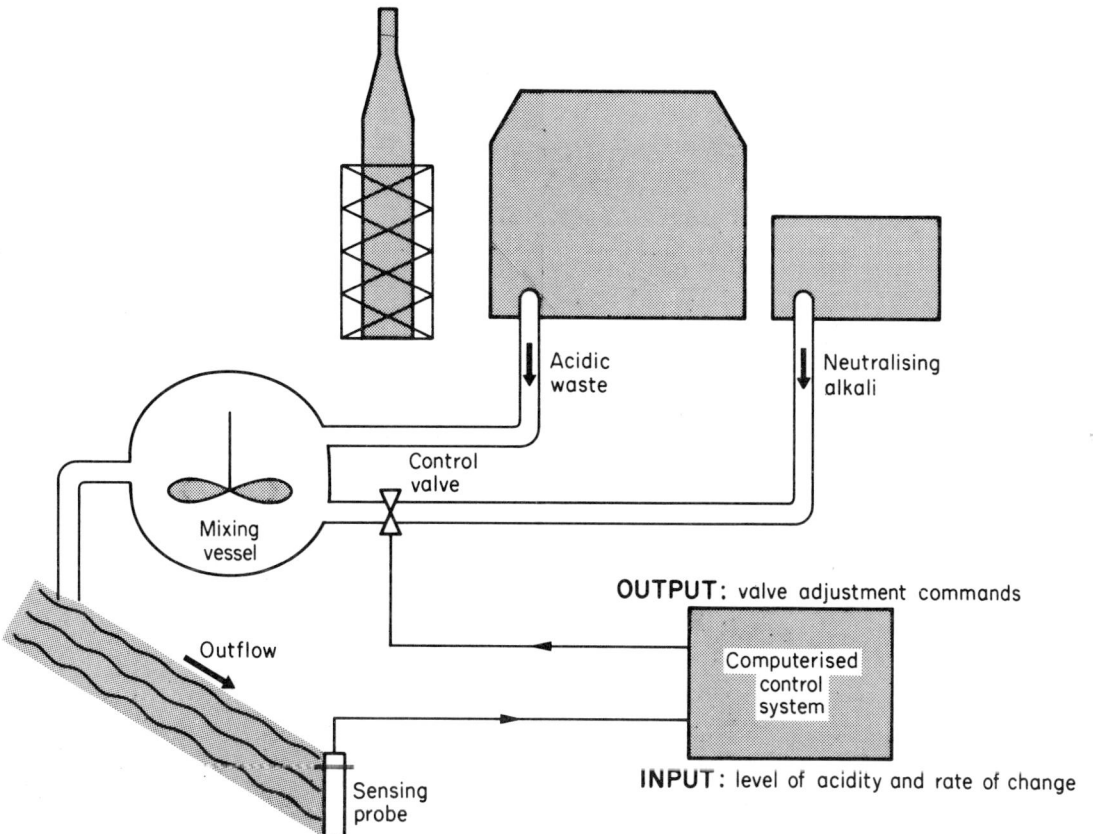

Fig. 2.8 A simplified system for the control of effluent from a chemical plant.

effluent-control system would have instruments measuring the flow rates of effluent and neutralising agent as well as the acidity of the mixture downstream. In response to a rise in acidity downstream the computer might control an increase in alkali flow rate, carefully monitoring that excess expensive alkali is not illegally discharged. Such systems can be very sophisticated, measuring not only current values but rates of change in the values and cumulative factors, and exercising control according to complex calculations involving these factors. Key to such systems are devices to convert the analogue instrument readings into digital form, and devices to control analogue outputs (e.g. valve settings) from digital instructions issued by the computer.

(h) The immediate future

It is worth mentioning two trends which seem likely to have a major impact on computer input within a few years. These are the high rates of electronic data transfer and decrease in computer storage costs that technology is achieving. Two input media seem likely to capitalise on these trends.

(i) Voice input. Digitised speech input could reduce much of the labour content of data input. Particularly promising is the area of message switching in which the ease of input would encourage use, and where no complicated interpretation of the data is required from the computer.

(ii) Bit-image processing. This is the breaking down of the image of any document, including, for example, diagrams and handwritten text, into digitised form. Its economical storage and retrieval in a form similar to that of a television picture would be more attractive than existing clumsy optical and magnetic character recognition methods.

Exercises 2

1 For the system used in Exercises 1, question 1, what input/output devices do you think it uses and why?
2 Describe a real or imaginary (science fiction included) sensing and controlling device. What factors would it need to measure, and how would it calculate its response?
3 For the system used in Exercises 1, question 3, what input/output devices would you recommend and why?
4 Describe in your own words the main features of a computer's structure and way of working.
5 An aircraft seat-booking system is to be designed for use in travel agencies. Explain what input/output devices you would recommend (think of devices required centrally as well as any local devices).

3 Computer Software

3.1 Types of computer program

Software is the general term for any set of instructions which have been properly formulated so that when they are set up on a suitable medium, they can direct a computer's activities. Such a set of instructions is called a computer program. The instructions are formulated according to the rules of a computer-programming language (about which more will be said) and take the form of lines of text, perhaps with a few special symbols or mnemonic codes (e.g. STR to represent the process of SToRing a value in a particular location).

(a) Applications programs

Programs which are designed to carry out tasks which arise directly from applying the computer to a problem external to the computer centre, are called applications programs. Examples of applications software are payroll programs (to read in employee details and hours worked, to calculate pay, and to read out the results), design programs (to calculate the dimensions of an item required to be capable of a certain performance specification), and any other program designed to perform an external business, technical or educational function.

(b) Utility programs

Arising from the need to process applications programs, there is a need for another type of software called utility programs. These programs are required to perform functions which are common to the operation of many different applications programs. Examples are: programs to sort data into alphabetical or numerical sequence; programs to duplicate data held on magnetic tape or disk; and programs to delete data so that magnetic disks can be efficiently reused.

(c) Software packages

Programs are often grouped together to form a suite of programs to tackle several aspects of an application, and these may well be written in a generalised way so that individual users may run the software, choosing a particular set of options or parameters to suit them. For example a payroll program may allow the user to select from a range of pension fund deduction rules, and may have some associated programs such as one to allow a new employee's name etc. to be added to the file of employee details. It is common to refer to such software as a package, and there are many software packages on the market providing, for example, payroll, stock-control or word-processing functions. A software package will normally be provided with supporting user documentation explaining its facilities, and will have the programs stored on magnetic tape or disk. Software packages have economic attractions because it is usually cheaper to buy a suitable package (if one can be found) than to have a program specially written for a particular task. The factors affecting the design and selection of two types of application package often used on micro computer systems are discussed in Section 3.5.

(d) Operating systems and multi-programming

A computer's operating system consists of software supplied by the computer manufacturer, which is 'booted' in on occasions when the machine is started up, and under the control of which the computer always operates. The operating system ensures that the facilities of the machine are co-ordinated so as to make optimum use of the system. This includes controlling the various input and output devices, and the allocation of storage to programs and their data.

In mainframe or minicomputers multi-programming is nearly always employed and this involves the storage and execution of several programs at the same time. The benefit of multi-programming is that different parts of the computer system can be used by different programs at the same time, for example allowing calculation on one program to take place whilst another is using an input device to obtain data. The operating system and the use of multi-programming thus ensure efficient use of all the computer's components and peripherals.

3.2 Types of computer programming languages

Many languages exist to allow computer programmers to instruct their machines to carry out their required tasks. The differences between various languages arise out of two main factors:
- (i) the emphasis put on the ease of writing as opposed to the speed with which the computer will be able to execute or carry out the instructions of the program;
- (ii) the type of application that the program is to be used for i.e. technical, commercial and general purpose or specialised.

The first factor dominates the categorisation of programming languages, and has led to the terms 'high level' and 'low level' which are used to describe them.

(a) High-level languages

High-level languages are those which provide a high level of resemblance to natural language and mathematical notation. They allow a programmer to create complex programs with the minimum of difficulty, because the program statements are so similar to the normal methods of writing down instructions. The only disadvantage of this type of programming language is the relatively slow speed with which it can be processed by a computer, which can lead to higher machine operating costs. The most common examples of high-level languages are BASIC, FORTRAN, COBOL, PL/1 and ALGOL. Of these COBOL and PL/1 are business orientated, while FORTRAN and ALGOL are suited to technical applications. BASIC is used in both technical and business applications. They are all fairly general-purpose languages within their field of application: some specialised high-level languages exist for specific purposes such as simulation or the manipulation of large tables of numbers in matrix form.

(b) Low-level languages

Low-level languages have a low level of resemblance to natural language, and will often require several statements to achieve what a high-level language could encapsulate in one statement. They tend to use mnemonic codes and to be limited to one simple operation per line. As a consequence such programs are difficult for a programmer to write and for anyone else to understand, but they do have the advantage that they are more easily processed by a computer. Each of the computer manufacturers tend to have their own low-level language, which can be used for either technical or commercial applications because of the fundamental nature of its instructions. However it is fair to say that technical programs tend to be written in high-level languages because they make the most efficient use of their authors' time and because technical programmers are often well-qualified and highly-paid technicians. Low-level languages are sometimes called assembly-level languages.

3.3 Compilation and execution

A common practice is for a program written in a high-level or low-level language, the source program, to be compiled or assembled into an object program which consists of strings of instructions in machine code, i.e. the binary digits 0 and 1. This compilation is carried out once only by a utility program called a compiler. Once compiled the object program can then be executed efficiently every time the program is required. If program amendments are to be made however they must be made to the source program, which will then have to be re-compiled to produce a new object program (see Figure 3.1).

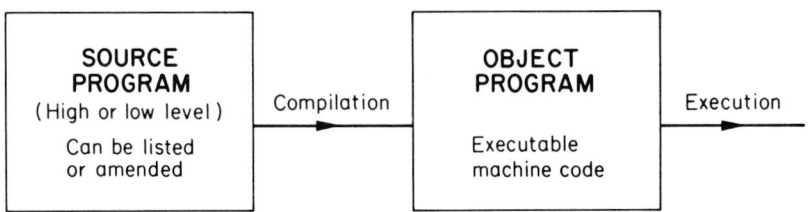

Fig. 3.1 The process of compilation.

3.4 Interpreters

An alternative practice to compiling the source program and executing the object program is to interpret the source program into machine code line by line as it is executed. This approach is most often used when a program is being created on-line from a terminal, so that each line is checked for correct syntax, only being accepted as a valid statement if the check has been successful. The majority of computer systems using the BASIC language process their BASIC programs interpretively, as shown in Figure 3.2.

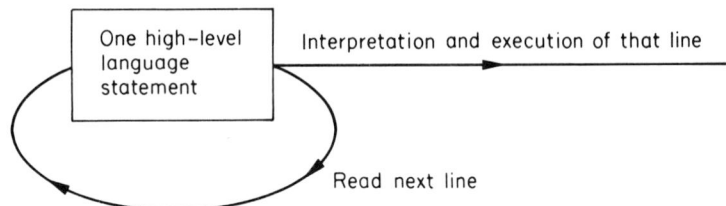

3.5 Using software packages

When software packages to perform some task are being selected, there are a number of features which need to be considered. The cost of the package is very rarely an important factor in choosing between alternatives. Much more critical are the questions of how nearly a package meets your needs, and whether the package and your computer are capable of handling the task effectively. In this section we consider two case studies to illustrate exactly what is involved.

(a) Case study 1—a file management package

Consider a medium-sized factory with a large number of items of electrical equipment requiring regular maintenance and testing. What is the likelihood that a computerised filing system could provide genuine benefits to the factory in handling the records associated with the equipment? The most obvious applications would be the quick retrieval and updating of details concerning any particular item, the ability to generate lists of items requiring routine maintenance in a given time period and the ability to select and list any items of equipment having some particular property, e.g. all lathes from a certain manufacturer. Let us assume that the electrical engineers have access to a microcomputer system with a twin 12.7 cm floppy disk drive, with 200K bytes of storage capacity on each disk.

(i) Will the computer hardware do the job? Suppose that there are 500 items for which details should be recorded and that information is required in the categories shown in Table 3.1. It is

Table 3.1

Data	Number of characters
Works' identification number	10
Type of equipment	15
Manufacturer	15
Year of manufacture	4
Purchase cost (£)	7
Voltage	3
Power rating (kW)	3
Inspection interval (weeks)	3
Site location code	5
Date of last five inspections	30 (6 ×5)
Comments on last five inspections	100 (20 ×5)
Total number of characters per item	195

likely that this type of floppy disk will employ blocks or sectors of 256 characters or $\frac{1}{4}$K bytes, so that it is sensible to assume that one item's details should be stored per block (this also allows for extra information as the system develops, always a wise policy). Since there are some 500 items we will require some $500 \times \frac{1}{4}$K bytes of storage capacity, i.e. 125K bytes, and this will fit conveniently, with some room for an increase in the number of electrical items, on one 200K disk. If we had required up to half a dozen disks the system would still have been manageable by using separate disks to hold information either for different types of equipment or for items stored in different parts of the factory. Processing may then have involved loading several disks in succession. Above half a dozen or so disks this system would have become unwieldy, and different hardware would have to be considered. Processing time on such a small system can be dismissed as the microcomputer would be capable of reading the entire disk in a matter of a few minutes.

(ii) Will the software package be flexible enough? The first question to be levelled at any package being considered for this application is, 'Can it handle the groups of information (known as data fields) for each item's record?'. The ease with which the format of the records can be created (and amended if changes are thought to be necessary) is a consideration. Similarly the ease with which the details in the records themselves can be set-up and amended is important. In particular consider the data fields representing the last five inspections. These are an example of repeated fields, and how the package handles them will say a lot for its sophistication. If each field in this group has to be specified individually and laboriously, and if it is up to the user to do the necessary housekeeping to ensure that the latest data always go into the correct field, then the package will obviously be less attractive than one which handles such things automatically.

The general ease with which the operation of the package can be learnt, and with which updating and selection of records for display can be achieved, is very important. A clumsy package which is difficult to comprehend will soon be rejected by its intended users. It is important to know whether searches are limited to simple matches of character or strings of numbers, or whether combinations of matches can be used (such as all lathes purchased from a certain manufacturer before a given year). Similarly the ability of the package to derive certain simple totals is important, e.g. as well as identifying all items satisfying the conditions of the previous sentence, can the package total their gross purchase prices? It is likely that hard-copy (printed) output would be required, and the ease with which well designed output reports could be produced from a printer would be of interest. Finally the extent to which the problems of storage 'back-up' had been considered, to cater for failure or loss of the memory, would be important, and to a lesser extent the question of what facilities existed for inserting validity checks into the numeric data fields (e.g. range limits outside which data is rejected at the input stage).

(b) Case study 2 — a calculation package

(i) The problem. Consider Table 3.2 which represents in simplified form the type of calculation that is necessary to evaluate the economic worth of a project, for example the installation of a large item of industrial plant. The rows of numbers represent expenditure that is planned (negative by convention) and forecast revenues to be generated by the project. The columns define the years in which the flows of cash are to take place. The sum total of revenues minus expenditure gives the net cash flow

Table 3.2 Project cash flow table (values are in £ ×1000)

	Column	1 yr1	2 yr2	3 yr3	4 yr4	5 yr5	6 yr6	7 Total
row 1	Capital costs	−100						−100
2	Maintenance costs	−10	−20	−20	−30	−30	−30	−140
3	Site overheads	−5	−5	−5	−6	−6	−6	−33
4	Product A revenues	10	15	20	30	50	30	155
5	Product B revenues		10	15	20	20	20	85
6	Product C revenues		10	10	10	10	10	50
7	Product D revenues		10	10	20	10		50
8	Net cash flow	−105	20	30	44	54	24	67
9	Discounted cash flow (at 10% per annum rate)	−95.5	16.5	22.5	30.1	33.5	13.5	**20.6**

for each year. A discounted value is calculated by dividing by the factor

$$\left(1 + \frac{r}{100}\right)^n$$

where r is the percentage discounting rate per annum and n is the number of years since the project was begun. Finally a total for each row is calculated, giving a net total discounted cash flow for the entire project in the bottom right hand corner (in bold).

(ii) The requirements of a package. Software packages exist to handle calculations involving any type of tables. Their attraction is that the rules defining the meaning of the rows and columns can be set up when the program is run, including rules for deriving values in one row or column from expressions involving values in one or more others. The other major attraction is the ability to re-calculate the entire table if any data assumptions are changed. Some of the factors to be considered in appraising such packages are listed below.

- How easy is it to set up, alter and store the row and column name definitions?
- How big a table can the package deal with?
- How flexible is the definition of the relationship between rows and columns (e.g. can it deal with dividing by the factor $\left(1 + \frac{r}{100}\right)^n$ in which n is different for each column)?
- How easy is it to re-calculate the table if some data are amended?
- What facilities exist for storing and printing the calculated table?
- How easy is it to display the data on the terminal/microcomputer screen? (Some packages allow the screen to act as a 'window' on large tables, allowing them to be moved to display the desired rows and columns.)

- How easy is it to learn to use the package, and how easy is it to operate in normal situations?

Packages like this can be used by non-programmers, avoiding the need for expensive tailor-made programs to be written for each separate application, thus saving many times their purchase price. The standard of such software is now generally good in the mini and mainframe computer application areas, but it is more variable where microcomputer packages are involved simply because the technology is new, developing fast, and more open to unlicensed software copying.

Exercises 3

1. Explain the difference between high- and low-level programming languages. If a medium-sized industrial firm has a policy of keeping mainframe-computer hardware costs low and has surplus staff that it could redeploy as programmers, which level of programming language would you recommend and why?
2. Describe the purpose of a compiler, and the meaning of the terms source and object as applied to computer programs.
3. Imagine that you have a microcomputer file-management software package, and a system including floppy-disk storage. Describe a filing and retrieval task that you might use the package for, saying what data fields (and their lengths in characters) you might use. Describe also the type of searches that you might find useful. Would it be practicable to store the volume of data that your application would require on floppy disks?
4. Describe the difference between applications and utility packages giving two examples of each.
5. The Look Ahead Engineering Company have asked you to draw up a series of cost estimates for manufacturing an item which can be constructed to five possible design specifications using different components as shown by ● in the table below

Components	V	W	Design X	Y	Z
A	●	●	●	●	
B	●		●	●	●
C			●		●
D	●	●	●	●	
E				●	●
F	●				
G		●	●		

If additionally some of the components are imported and subject to exchange rate fluctuations, what use could you make of computers to provide the required cost estimates?

6. Describe the functions of an operating system.

 The BASIC Programming Language (I)

4.1 Introduction

There are many programming languages as described in Chapter 3, and BASIC is a good, high-level language for beginners and professionals alike to work with. There are many slightly different versions of this language in use but this book will deal primarily with the common main elements, indicating special features where appropriate. BASIC statements used in this book will work without any modification on Commodore computers. Simple examples will be given as the elements are introduced and some realistic program listings are given in later chapters, accompanied by explanations of the aspects of programming technique which they illustrate.

4.2 Arithmetic

Before discussing features particular to BASIC it is worth considering a problem which is common to all programming languages and to mathematical notation in general. As an example consider the expression $2+10/5$. Is this to be understood as $2+\frac{10}{5}$ or as $\frac{2+10}{5}$? In the former case the expression would have the value 4 whilst in the latter it would be 2.4, so it is clearly important that we have a definition. Now the rules adopted by BASIC and most other computer languages are simple and correspond to those rules which we have come to take for granted in ordinary arithmetic. The rules involve giving a different level of priority to the four fundamental functions of addition, subtraction, multiplication and division, as well as to the operation of raising a number to a power (called exponentiation and represented by the symbol ↑ as in 3↑2 for 3^2).

The rules are:
 (i) expressions in brackets are evaluated first, with operations then being carried out in descending priority order;
 (ii) where operations have equal priority the leftmost one is evaluated first.

The priorities are:
 (i) highest level   ↑ raising to powers;

(ii) intermediate level   *, / multiplication and division;
(iii) lowest level   +, − addition and subtraction.

In passing we note that an asterisk is used for multiplication to avoid confusion with the letter 'X'.

For example in the expression 2 + 10/5 we have to evaluate the 10/5 part first because division has the higher priority level, and only then is addition applied to arrive at the correct answer of 4. If we have the expression (2 + 10)/5 to evaluate then our rules tell us that the brackets must be evaluated first giving us 12 to divide by 5, i.e. 2.4.

As exercises verify the following.

(i)   6 − 3 + 5   = 8   (iv)   3 * 2 + 5   = 11
(ii)   6 − (3 + 5) = −2   (v)   4/(5 * 3 − 13) = 2
(iii)   3 + 2 ↑ 3   = 11   (vi)   3/5 * 4   = 2.4

As a final practical point notice that an expression like

$$3 * 2 \uparrow 5 + 3/5 * 4$$

is quite unambiguous and acceptable to a computer. However it is much clearer for a human trying to comprehend it if brackets are introduced thus,

$$(3 * (2 \uparrow 5)) + ((3/5) * 4)$$

The use of brackets as an aid to the comprehension of your program listings by yourself and other people is therefore strongly recommended.

4.3 BASIC programs

A BASIC program is a series of instructions, each uniquely identified by a line number and executed in increasing line number order. For example one of the simplest instructions is the PRINT instruction, which causes words or numbers to be printed out or displayed (depending on the hardware used). A three line BASIC program using the PRINT instruction is

```
10 PRINT "THE ANSWER IS"
20 PRINT 2 + 10/5
30 END
```

Notice that the line numbers 10, 20, 30 have been chosen so that there is opportunity to insert additional line numbers if required at a later stage either before line 10, between lines 10 and 20, or between lines 20 and 30. Notice too that the zeros have been shown with a line through them, this is conventional and distinguishes the zero from the letter 'O', a common source of problems for the novice programmer. When this program is loaded into a computer we need only type RUN and press the

RETURN key for its execution to start. Line 10 will cause the text 'THE ANSWER IS' to be printed out, whilst line 20 will cause the group of numbers 2 + 10/5 to be evaluated and then the answer 4 to be printed out. Line 30 is simply a statement to tell the computer to stop processing this program. It is worth noting in passing that this program could have been written in two lines as

 10 PRINT "THE ANSWER IS"; 2 + 10/5
 20 END

where the semicolon is used to separate the two items to be printed. The semicolon will generate about two or three spaces between the items, depending on the type of machine being used, whereas a comma, which could have been used as an alternative, would generate about five or six spaces between them. We could construct several different programs along similar lines to the one above, but they would all suffer from an obvious limitation; we have not yet learnt of a way to make our program run with different data, so that it is not simply limited to performing the same calculation with the same answer every time we run it. In order to overcome this limitation two things are needed, an instruction for putting in variable data to the computer, and a way of manipulating that data once it has been entered.

4.4 Variables and the INPUT instruction

In computer programming, variables can be thought of as pigeon-holes used to store data. We will limit our thinking to numbers for the moment (leaving words for the next chapter), and can think of the number 132 for example being stored in one such pigeon-hole. Each pigeon-hole must have some identification so that the computer can decide which pigeon-hole we are interested in, and this identification is effectively the variable name. We can imagine then how the number 132 can be set up as the contents of a particular pigeon-hole, and that we can refer to the contents in some calculation without changing the number stored there. Eventually we may wish to store a different number there, in which case the previous contents are completely overwritten. The rules for naming variables in BASIC are:
 (i) a simple numeric variable name can be any letter or a letter followed by a number;
 (ii) most versions of BASIC allow extensions to the above definition. Some allow two letters, a few allow even more and some allow up to six characters to be used (for clarity of program interpretation) but only in fact take heed of the first two characters, so that TOTAL and TOLL, say, would be regarded as the same variable.

As guidance in selecting variable names it is strongly recommended that they be chosen so as to have meaningful forms which are easily remembered and understood. For example: T for a total; T1 and T2 when two temperatures, say, are involved; C for cost; IR for interest rate.

Although it is superficially attractive there are practical difficulties with using longer variable names even if they are allowed by a particular system because:

    (i) they increase the amount of key punching effort needed to set up a program;

    (ii) they increase the main memory or RAM storage required to hold the program;

    (iii) they allow more scope for key punching mistakes, leading to program errors;

    (iv) there is the danger of variables like TOTAL and TOLL getting muddled;

    (v) arithmetic expressions involving long names can actually be harder to comprehend than those with simpler names, for example $U*T+0.5*F*T\uparrow2$ compared with $INITSP*TIME+0.5*ACCEL*TIME\uparrow2$.

However when short names are used a document listing variable names and what factors they represent is an essential requirement.

The INPUT instruction allows the computer to ask for data, and

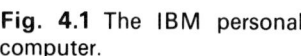

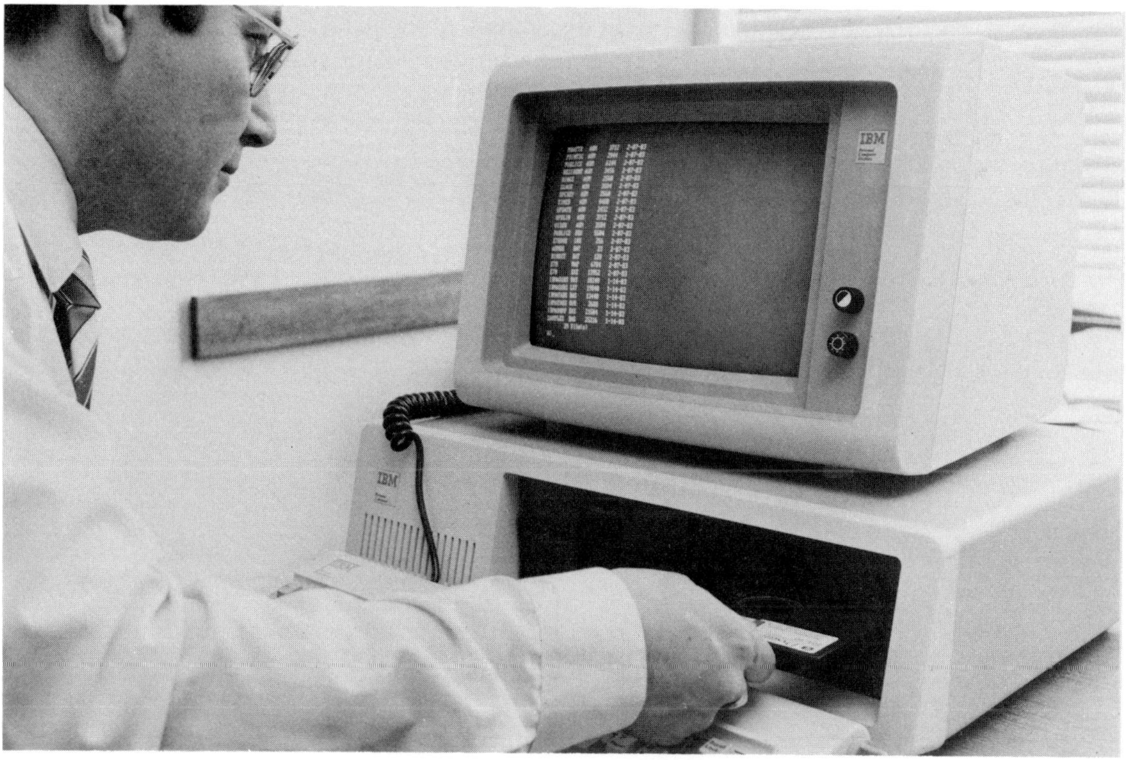

Fig. 4.1 The IBM personal computer.

also defines which variable names they are to be assigned to. A general example of an INPUT instruction is

    20 INPUT X, Y, Z

This tells the computer to expect three numbers to be input from the keyboard (separated by commas) and to allocate these numbers to the variables X, Y and Z. We can now write a more useful sort of program. Let's take as an example the calculation of the volume of a rectangular box.

    10 PRINT "TYPE IN LENGTH, HEIGHT, WIDTH IN CM"
    20 INPUT L, H, W
    30 PRINT "VOLUME (CC.) IS"; L*H*W
    40 END

We can run this program as many times as we like and use different figures for length, height and width each time. In each case the computer will invite us, with a single question mark at the start of a new printer or screen line, to input our list of data. The INPUT statement can have as many variables as will fit on one line. If there is only one variable involved then there is no need to have a comma.

4.5 The LET instruction

The calculation of volume in the last example was accomplished in a PRINT statement, but this is not always convenient and it is often necessary or clearer to calculate the results at an intermediate stage. The LET instruction is used for this purpose and an example is

    25 LET V = L*H*W

This instruction assigns the value evaluated for the right-hand expression to the variable V, which can then be printed if desired. To give a further example let us look at a program to convert temperatures expressed in degrees Centigrade to degrees Fahrenheit. (Remember the rule for this is: multiply by 9, divide by 5 and add 32.)

    10 PRINT "ENTER CENTIGRADE TEMPERATURE"
    20 INPUT C
    30 LET F = C*9/5+32
    40 PRINT C; "CENTIGRADE = "; F; "FAHRENHEIT"
    50 END

The LET instruction can be abbreviated by omitting the word LET, so that

    25 V = L*H*W

or

30 F = C * 9/5 + 32

are valid alternatives to the previous two examples. For brevity professional programmers use the abbreviated form and it does no harm to use it from the outset, provided that whenever an equals sign is encountered in this way it is understood to mean 'becomes equal to'.

4.6 The FOR .... NEXT loop

The conversion program above is clearly a very straightforward one; often, calculations are not simple evaluations of one formula for one set of data and a device which is frequently useful to the programmer is the FOR . . . . NEXT loop. Essentially this is an instruction which tells the computer to repeat a series of instructions a prescribed number of times, each time giving an updated value to the loop counter which keeps track of the number of times the instructions have been executed. The instructions which are to be repeated the prescribed number of times are bounded at the beginning (the lower statement number end) by a FOR statement, and at the end (the higher statement number end) by a NEXT statement. A simple example is

```
20 FOR I = 1 TO 10
 . . . . . other statements . . . . .
100 NEXT I
```

This would cause all statements between 20 and 100 to be executed 10 times, the first time with the variable I set equal to 1, the second time with I set to 2 and so on up to I set equal to 10. Let's look at a program to calculate the sum of the reciprocals of the first N integers, where N is a number which we will specify to the computer at run time.

```
10 PRINT "TYPE IN N"
20 INPUT N
30 T = 0
40 FOR J = 1 TO N
50 T = T + 1/J
60 NEXT J
70 PRINT
80 PRINT "SUM OF RECIPROCALS OF FIRST"; N; "INTEGERS = "; T
```

Line 10 is a simple PRINT instruction which will display the text 'TYPE IN N' either on our screen or printer. Line 20 will produce a question mark inviting us to key in the number we wish the computer to use for its calculation. Line 30 says 'T becomes equal to zero', T will be used here as a running total and this means that it must be set to zero at the outset. (Some machines assume initial values of zero for all variables which have not been given values, but as a practical point it is easier for someone else looking at your program to spot where you initialise a variable than to look through your entire program satisfying themselves that you have left it to the machine to initialise it with a zero value.) Lines 40 and 60 define the boundaries of a FOR .... NEXT loop and the lines in between (in this case just line 50) are repeated N times, first with J = 1, secondly with J = 2 etc. up to J = N. Now it is worth noting that the loop variable (J in this case) can be any valid variable name and that the loop limits (1 and N here) can be any constants or expressions involving variables. Line 50 in fact calculates 1/J and adds it into the running total T. Line 70 merely produces a blank line on the screen or printer to help clarity by separating the display of the input from the display of the results. Line 80 produces a suitably annotated answer by giving the final value of the running total T. A FOR ... NEXT loop may contain another FOR .... NEXT loop within itself, but the loop variables must of course be different. FOR .... NEXT loops are not allowed to overlap.

As a final point here about FOR .... NEXT loops it is necessary to point out that most machines allow some sophistication in the increments by which the loop variable changes. In this way the loop variable may be made to take values like 1, 4, 7, 10, 13, 16 etc. or 67, 62, 57, 52, 47, 42 etc. However in the author's experience where such values are required it is nearly always beneficial to keep to a simple FOR definition and to use a statement like $I1 = 3*I - 2$ or $J1 = 72 - 5*J$ immediately after the FOR statement. The advantage is that the structure of the number sequence is made obvious and if reference does ever have to be made to the number of times the loop has been executed then the loop variables are available for that task.

4.7 The GOTO instruction

This instruction provides a way of jumping out of the normal ascending line number sequence of processing instructions to a specified statement number. When a GOTO instruction is encountered this specified statement will be executed next and processing will continue from that statement. For example the program

```
10 PRINT "ENTER A NUMBER"
20 INPUT N
30 PRINT "SQUARE ROOT OF"; N; "IS"; N↑0.5
40 GOTO 10
```

will ask the user to enter a number, it will calculate and suitably print the square root of that number and then ask for another number and repeat the process in an endless loop until the break key is pressed to jump out of the program. If this were all that could be achieved the GOTO instruction would not be worth mentioning, but it becomes very necessary and powerful when used in combination with the IF instruction described next.

4.8 The IF instruction

The IF instruction enables the computer to test the truth of an expression involving variables and to transfer execution to a specified statement if the expression is true. For example consider the line of code below.

    30 IF A = 3 THEN 100

This would transfer execution to line 100 if A = 3, but would otherwise just execute the next line after line 30. As a further example let's go back to our degrees Centigrade to degrees Fahrenheit conversion program and insert the following lines.

    42 IF F > 212 THEN 48
    44 PRINT "THIS IS NOT ABOVE BOILING POINT"
    46 GOTO 50
    48 PRINT "THIS IS ABOVE BOILING POINT"

Here the IF and GOTO instructions ensure that an appropriate message is printed out. In particular notice that the GOTO instruction in line 46 is necessary to avoid printing both messages out when F is less than or equal to 212. Also be on the lookout for situations which do not require a GOTO, so that your programs are not unnecessarily long and complex. For example if we only required a message when F was greater than 212 then we could use the following lines instead of lines 42-48.

    41 IF F <= 212 THEN 50
    49 PRINT "THIS IS ABOVE BOILING POINT"

Notice that these lines did not require a GOTO instruction, and note also that the combination of less than and equals signs denotes the 'less than or equal to' condition. In fact IF instructions can become quite sophisticated using the terms 'AND' and 'OR' and '< >' for not equal to, hence the following examples would be valid lines of code.

    50 IF A > B AND C = D THEN 20

or

    130 IF A >= 3 OR B < 2 THEN 250

or

    40 IF (A + B)/C > 1.5 AND D = 2 THEN 60

Even more complex forms are possible but it is advisable for clarity to try and keep IF statements simple, using several if necessary in order to keep the logic obvious.

4.9 A sample program—time series

To illustrate the use of the BASIC instructions described in this chapter, a sample program is provided below. Although later chapters deal more fully with the process of devising program logic some discussion is given here to help the understanding of the program structure. The program is designed to produce a 'time series' which is literally a series of values of some specific factor at regular time intervals, where the value at a given time is dependent upon its value in the previous time period. For example there are sensible grounds for regarding the size of a population of animals or people as being dependent on the population size in the previous year. Other examples might be the sales of a product from year to year or even the production costs. The program assumes a relationship of the form:

$$NEW = A(OLD)^B + C$$

where NEW, OLD are new and old values respectively and A, B, C are constants which are to be specified.

We will see however that the form of this relationship could very easily be changed as it is defined in just one line of the program (line 210).

Firstly let us observe that our program will have four logical parts.

(i) Input. This is where constants like A, B, C are input to the computer.

(ii) Initialisation. This is where certain preparatory things are done, like the setting up of headings ready for the results to be printed or displayed underneath.

(iii) Calculation. A suprisingly small part of most programs, this is where the real meat of the calculation is carried out.

(iv) Termination. The tidying up after the job has been done.

The coding of the program is given below. The numbering sequence has gaps to indicate the logical split of the program into the above divisions and for clarity these have been set out with a blank line between them.

```
10 PRINT "PROGRAM TO CALCULATE A TIME SERIES"
20 PRINT "TYPE IN THE VALUES OF A, B, C"
30 INPUT A, B, C
40 PRINT "WHAT IS THE INITIAL VALUE"
50 INPUT V0
60 PRINT "HOW MANY TIME PERIODS ARE REQUIRED"
70 INPUT N
```

```
100 PRINT
110 PRINT "TIME VALUE"
120 PRINT
130 PRINT 0, V0
140 V = V0

200 FOR I = 1 TO N
210 V = A * V ↑ B + C
220 IF V > 10 ↑ 6 OR V < -10 ↑ 6 THEN 250
230 PRINT I, V
240 GOTO 270
250 PRINT I, "VALUE OUT OF RANGE"
260 GOTO 300
270 NEXT I

300 PRINT
400 END
```

The following comments deal with each line, or group of lines, in turn.

Line(s)	Comments
10	This prints a title to show clearly which program this is, and on machines which give the option should include a code to make the machine start with a clear screen or a new page.
20–30	These capture the three constant factors at the same time. Depending on the intended users for this program it is worth considering including a display of the formula describing the part that A, B and C play in it.
40–50	These specify the initial value separately as it is logically different from the other factors. If V had been used for this variable then it would not be possible in some development of this program to refer to the initial value after the other values had been calculated.
60–70	N is the standard variable name for this type of variable
100	It is a good idea to separate input from output by at least one blank line.
110–120	These prepare headings and a space beneath them (column width is best judged by trial and error, it will depend on the characteristics of your machine). More sophisticated alignment is discussed in later chapters.
130	This prints the initial value as a reference.
140	This initialises V in preparation for its use in the calculation.

200	This is the start of the calculation loop, I is another standard variable name for this sort of task.
210	Note that V 'becomes equal to' an expression involving its previous value.
220	This tests, using the IF instruction, for situations where the numeric value is in danger of becoming impractically high or low.
230	This prints a line for the time period currently being considered.
240	This GOTO statement ensures that the time period loop counter is consulted next. Note that this is necessary to avoid statements 250 and 260.
250–260	These print an out of range message if appropriate, and cause a jump out of the calculation process to end the program prematurely.
270	This is the end of the FOR .... NEXT loop, and increments the value of I by 1 before returning to line 200 to test whether N has been exceeded or not.
300	It is a good idea to leave at least one blank line after the program results have been printed or displayed.
400	This is the END statement, which is not always essential depending on machine, but is a useful indicator that this is the end of the program (especially for multi-page or multi-screen listings).

Exercises 4

1 Write a BASIC program to evaluate and display the polynomial

$$AX^4 + BX^3 + CX^2 + DX + E$$

for integer values of X from 1 to 10, where A, B, C, D and E are constants to be input at run time.

2 Devise two similar but different time series to that shown in Section 4.9, with the values in each series being expressions including the last term in the other series. (A real example might be the populations of two types of animal, one of which was a predator.) Write a BASIC program to display the terms of the two time series.

3 Newton's Method is an example of what is called an iterative technique, where successive approximations are made to a required solution, each using the previous estimate and being more accurate than it. To find a cube root for example, Newton's Method gives the formula

$$\text{next estimate} = X - \frac{(X^3 - A)}{3X^2}$$

where X is the previous estimate and A is the number whose cube root is to be calculated. Write a BASIC program to find the cube root of a number using Newton's Method, with the number and the first estimate of the root being given as input. Choose an appropriate small difference such as 0.001 between successive approximations as a criterion for ending the program and printing the best estimate. Compare this method with the expression A ↑ (1/3). Why do you think the computer can evaluate this expression faster than executing your program?

4 The discounted cash flow for a business project takes account of interest rates to decrease or discount the value given to incomes or expenditures which occur in some year in the future. A sum S occurring in n years time assuming a discounting rate of r% per year is given a discounted value of

$$\frac{S}{(1 + r/100)^n}$$

Write a computer program to calculate the total discounted cash flow for a project over a number of years, with the annual incomes or expenditures and the rate of discount as the input.

5 Write a BASIC program to calculate the sum of the squares of the first N integers, where N is to be the input. As a check also make your program evaluate the formula

$$\frac{N(N+1)(2N+1)}{6}$$

6 A quadratic equation $AX^2 + BX + C = 0$ has roots given by

$$\frac{-B \pm \sqrt{B^2 - 4AC}}{2A}$$

Write a BASIC program to calculate the roots, given A, B and C as the input. If $B^2 < 4AC$ the roots are imaginary. Devise a way of coping with this and the case where $B^2 = 4AC$.

5 The BASIC Programming Language (II)

5.1 String variables

So far we have only considered variables which have numeric values. It is often necessary to use variables to hold textual data, i.e. strings of letters, or a mixture of letters and numbers. The rules for naming string variables are the same as those for numeric variables given in Section 4.4, with the exception that a $ is used after the first one or two letters of the variable name to signify its string nature. For example, A$, C3$, and CN$ are all valid string-variable names. The following simple program, which asks for the computer user's name and then responds with a personalised message, illustrates the usefulness of string variables.

```
10 PRINT "WHAT IS YOUR NAME"
20 INPUT N$
30 PRINT
40 PRINT "HELLO "N$" I'M YOUR"
50 PRINT "FRIENDLY PERSONAL COMPUTER!"
```

There are two points to be made from this example: firstly, string variables can be used in input and output statements in the same way as numeric variables; and secondly, for a neat screen-output display, notice how a blank was included in the fixed titles either side of N$ in line 40. A comma or semicolon could have been used to separate N$ from the titles in this line, but the result (several spaces between the name and the rest of the text) would not have been as professional. We could extend this example with the lines:

```
60 PRINT
70 PRINT "DO YOU WANT THAT REPEATED (Y OR N)"
80 INPUT A$
90 IF A$="Y" THEN 30
```

These extra statements illustrate the use of a string variable in an IF statement, for controlling the operation of a program. Notice particularly that the comparison required the quotes to be in place around the letter Y in line 90. A straightforward comparison between two string variables would not require any quotation marks.

5.2 Some string functions

It is in the area of string functions (i.e. functions for manipulating string variables) that there is the greatest discrepancy between the different manufacturers' versions of BASIC. For simplicity in this section the functions described apply to Commodore PET computers, but the differences between machines are not large.

(a) The MID$ function

The manipulation of a string variable to use just part of the string can be achieved using the MID$ function. For example the statement

```
50 PRINT MID$(B$,3,5)
```

will print 5 characters out of the 'middle' of the string variable B$ starting at the third character. As a further example consider the program statements below.

```
10 D$="MONTUEWEDTHUFRISATSUN"
15 T=0
20 FOR I=1 TO 7
30 D=3*I−2
40 PRINT "INPUT RAINFALL FOR "MID$(D$,D,3)
50 INPUT R
60 T=T+R
70 NEXT I
80 PRINT "AV. DAILY RAINFALL IS";T/7
```

Within the FOR .... NEXT loop the use of MID$ in line 40 will result in the correct abbreviation for each day of the week appearing in the request for the input of that day's rainfall. Notice in particular the numeric variable D, which being set to $3*I-2$, takes the values 1,4,7,10,13,16 and 19 as desired for the starting point of the required substring, as the loop variable I increases from 1 to 7. This form of 'number magic' becomes second nature with just a little practice, and has applications throughout the programming field. Finally, on this example, notice that the numeric variable D can be used without confusion with the string variable D$.

(b) Changing a string variable

The MID$ function can be used to modify the contents of a string. For example, suppose that we have the following piece of code,

```
100 P$−"TOTAL PRODUCTION LAST MONTH"
110 PRINT P$,T1
```

and that we wish to print a similar line for this month's production (held in the numeric variable T2). We could use MID$ to modify P$ as follows.

    120 P$ = MID$(P$,1,17) + "THIS" + MID$(P$,22,6)
    130 PRINT P$,T2

Of course we could have achieved this particular task in simpler ways with two PRINT statements containing both texts, but this example does illustrate a facility that can be very useful in more complicated situations. In general strings can be built up from other strings using statements like

    200 D$ = A$ + B$ + C$

The process of joining strings like this is called concatenation. One thing to look out for, when joining strings like this, is to make sure that you don't forget about the blank spaces required between words.

(c) The STR$ and VAL functions

A function STR$ exists to convert a numeric variable value to a character string, for manipulation as text. This is very useful for arranging the display of tables of numbers which may have different numbers of digits or different numbers of decimal places. Its use is illustrated in the example

    150 A$ = STR$(N)
    160 PRINT MID$(A$,1,3)

Here the first three characters of a number are printed. A word of warning is required because most machines treat the sign of the number as the first character, with a blank being used for positive numbers and the usual − sign for negative numbers. The lines of code above will therefore result in the sign and then the first two digits of the number N being printed. The important point is that STR$ converts the number into a text string which can then be concatenated or modified as required.

    The VAL function has the opposite effect to STR$ and converts a string representation of a number into a numeric value on which arithmetic can be performed. An example is given below.

    10 N$ = "365"
    20 X = VAL(N$)
    30 Y = X/7
    40 PRINT Y

(d) String length and the LEN function

Strings can contain letters, numbers and any other keyboard characters up to a maximum length which depends on the machine, but which is usually 256 characters. It is sometimes necessary to determine the length of a string, most commonly when some re-design of the format of numbers is required following the use of the STR$ function. The function LEN determines the length of a string of characters, for example

```
10 D$="MONTUEWEDTHUFRISATSUN"
20 PRINT LEN(D$)
```

would result in the number 21 being printed, i.e. the number of characters in the string. More usefully, suppose we have some calculated result stored in a variable V with a value between 10.00 and 99.99 and that we wish to display it, truncated to two decimal places if necessary, in a table which allows us six characters. The following coding will meet the task (remember we must cope with numbers such as 75.3, 47.2394, 20, 59.93).

```
100 S$=STR$(V)
110 L=LEN(S$)
120 IF L=6 THEN 300
130 IF L>6 THEN 200
140 REM*** L MUST BE <6 TO GET HERE
150 FOR I = 1 TO 6-L
160 REM*** ADD BLANKS TO START OF STRING
170 S$=" "+S$
180 NEXT I
190 GOTO 300
200 S$ = MID$(S$,1,6)
300 PRINT S$
```

Notice statement numbers 140 and 160 which are REMARK statements. These do not affect the program's execution but do serve to clarify a program listing. REM statements allow any comments, using any available characters, to be made. It is good practice to highlight the comments in some way so that they are easily spotted. In this example three asterisks have been used after the word REM, but the programmer may choose any method he likes.

5.3 Some other BASIC functions

(a) The INT function

Note that in this last example we have dealt with truncation, i.e. lopping off a few digits at the end of a number. It is appropriate here to mention a technique that can be used to achieve rounding, i.e. the process of quoting a number with accuracy to a given number of decimal places. For example, suppose we wish to round a numeric variable to one decimal place, then we may use the BASIC function INT, which has the property of calculating the integer part of a number, together with a little bit more number magic. E.g. INT(7.3) is 7 and INT(7.7) is 7. But note that

INT(7.3+0.5) is INT(7.8), i.e. 7, while INT(7.7+0.5) is INT(8.2), i.e. 8.

Now to use this technique to round a variable, V say, to one decimal place and print the result we may use the statement

150 PRINT INT(10*V+0.5)/10

For if V=7.33, then INT(73.3+0.5) yields 73, which in turn yields 7.3 when divided by 10. Similarly if V=7.37, then INT(73.7+0.5) yields 74, which in turn yields 7.4 when divided by 10.

(b) The ABS function

The ABS function calculates the absolute value of a numeric expression, i.e. it gives the magnitude of the value expressed as a positive number, regardless of whether or not the actual value is positive or negative. As an example of a situation in which this function is useful consider Exercises 4, question 3, in which successive approximations to a cube root are compared. If X1 and X2 are successive approximations, then the statement

200 IF ABS(X1−X2)<0.001 THEN 900

would detect when the absolute difference between X1 and X2 was less than 0.001 and jump to the appropriate part of the program, regardless of which of X1 and X2 is the larger.

(c) The RND function

A most useful function for games or more serious simulations is the RND function, which generates a random number expressed as a decimal between 0 and 1 (e.g. 0.5311028). The statement below illustrates the simplest use of this function.

50 PRINT RND(7)

The value 7 in brackets is known as a 'dummy argument' (a variable could have been used), and does not effect the random number generated as long as its value is positive. In some machines negative dummy arguments are used to generate a repeatable stream of pseudo-random numbers which we will not describe in detail here. Every time this statement is encountered a new random number between 0 and 1 will be printed. In practice we usually require our random numbers to fall into special ranges, and as an example consider the program below which can be used to draw selections for football pools forecasts!

```
 5 REM*** POOLS FORECAST PROGRAM
10 PRINT "HOW MANY SELECTIONS ARE REQUIRED"
20 INPUT S
30 PRINT "HOW MANY MATCHES ON THE COUPON"
40 INPUT N
```

The BASIC Programming Language (II) 53

Fig. 5.1 The DEC Rainbow personal computer.

```
50 PRINT
60 PRINT "YOUR"; S; "SELECTIONS ARE:—"
70 FOR I = 1 TO S
80 PRINT 1 + INT(N*RND(7))
90 NEXT I
```

It is line 80 which does all the work here, multiplying RND(7) by N and taking the integer part gives an integer in the range from 0 to N − 1, and adding one gives an integer in the desired range of 1 to N. The dummy argument 7 could be replaced by the reader's own lucky number, my only request is that should this program reap anyone a fortune then they will send 10% in my direction! On a more serious note it should be pointed out that this program is not sophisticated enough to check that there are no duplications in the numbers selected. To do this the selections would have to be stored as they are generated, and a comparison made with existing selections before a new one is accepted.

(d) Trigonometric and logarithmic functions

The following trigonometric and logarithmic functions are normally available:

SIN(X)—trigonometric sine of X (X expressed in radians),
COS(X)—cosine of X,
LOG(X)—natural or Naperian logarithm of X.

The function SQR(X) is also available which calculates the square root of X but which is just as effectively handled as X↑0.5.

(e) The TAB function

The TAB function is primarily designed to give control over the columns in which output is to be displayed on a screen. For example

10 PRINT TAB(10) "HELLO"

will display the word HELLO preceded by 10 blanks, i.e. starting in the eleventh column. Multiple use of TAB in one PRINT statement is valid as shown in the following statement

20 PRINT TAB(5) "THE TOTAL IS" TAB(19)X

here the text 'THE TOTAL IS' will appear starting in column 6 and the numeric value of X will be displayed starting in column 20. (Remember that when numbers are displayed the first character is reserved for the sign which is conventionally left blank when positive, so that the digits in this case will start in column 21.) TAB is a function which has been implemented in slightly different ways by different manufacturers. The above description is accurate for Commodore PET machines. Some other manufacturers interpret TAB(10) for example as determining that printing starts in the tenth as opposed to the eleventh column. A secondary aspect of the TAB function is its use for column control in printer output. Here no general rules can be given because of the diversity of the way in which different printers interpret the computer's commands. A way of controlling the print columns, which is independent of the machine being used, is to use a string of blanks, printing the required number by means of the MID$ function.

This completes the description of the most useful standard BASIC functions. The next chapter will complete our description of the BASIC language.

Exercises 5

1 Write a program which requests the user to give his name, address, occupation, and the year and month number of his birth. The program should calculate the user's age and display the data on the screen in the following format:

name IS A(N) occupation AGED y YEARS m MONTHS AND LIVES AT address.

The program should cope with printing 'AN' or 'A' depending on whether the user's occupation begins with a vowel or not.

2 Write a program which asks the user to enter a word, which determines the length of the word, and then randomly chooses one letter from the word to be replaced with a random letter from the alphabet, displaying the result and repeating this operation four more times.

```
              e.g. initial word TAPE
      computer produces ... TOPE
                             HOPE
                             HOLE
                             HALE
                             HALT
```

It is not required that all the combinations produced be valid words!

3 Write a program that calculates the volume and surface area of a ball bearing given its diameter in centimetres. (Use the formulae area = $4\pi r^2$ and volume = $\frac{4}{3}\pi r^3$ with π = 3.14159.) The output should be displayed rounded to four decimal places in the format illustrated below with the rightmost digits of the numbers vertically aligned and with trailing zeros being shown where appropriate.

```
SURFACE AREA IS     XX.XXXX SQUARE CM.
VOLUME IS           XX.XXXX CUBIC CM.
```

4 A machine tool produces components of average diameter 2.5 cm with an error which is equally likely to be anywhere in the range ± 0.05 cm. Write a program which simulates the random production process by producing diameters from the formula D = 2.5 + 0.1*(RND(7) − 0.5). Each diameter should be displayed when calculated and the program should stop with an appropriate message when a value greater than 2.545 or less than 2.455 is encountered.

continued overpage

5 As lunar module commander you have a readout as shown below.

HEIGHT	VELOCITY
(M)	(M/S)
±XXXXX	±XXXXX

This display is updated every second by your computer using the formulae

new height = old height − velocity + $\frac{1}{2}$K
new velocity = old velocity − K

where K is a factor reflecting the amount of retro-thrust being used, and velocities towards the lunar surface are regarded as positive. Write a program to calculate the new values of height and velocity given the old values and an input for K ensuring that they are displayed within the six character spaces allowed. (K is in units of ms^{-2} and you may like to know that the gravitational attraction of the moon can be taken as approximately $1.5\,ms^{-2}$ so that when your K factor is zero your rocket motors are actually producing $1.5\,ms^{-2}$ of thrust.)

6 Using the formulae of question 3 and assuming a density of $8\,g\,cm^{-3}$ write a BASIC program to tabulate diameter, surface area, volume and mass of ball bearings at diameter intervals of 0.1 cm from 0.5 cm to 2.0 cm. Ensure that the results maintain a strict columnar arrangement, with the leftmost digits being aligned for each column, and that the answers are given to three decimal places.

6 The BASIC Programming Language (III)

6.1 One-dimensional arrays

(a) Numeric arrays

It is frequently useful to be able to refer to variables as though they were items on a list, so that a single variable name can be used with a simple reference to the item's position in the list. For example if the numbers of items produced daily from a machine over a five-day period are to be analysed, a numeric-array variable P may be used with a label from 1 to 5 to identify which day's production is being referred to, so that P(3) say, holds the numeric value for the number of items produced on the third day. This way of referring to related items is particularly useful when repetitious operations are required, so that the full power of the FOR.... NEXT loop can be employed. The program below illustrates these points; it takes as input the 5 daily production figures and then tabulates them together with the figure expressed as a percentage of the total production over the five day period (to the nearest integer %).

```
10  T = 0
20  FOR I = 1 TO 5
30  PRINT "INPUT PRODUCTION FOR DAY"; I
40  INPUT P(I)
50  T = T + P(I)
60  NEXT I
70  PRINT
80  PRINT "DAY   PRODUCTION   % OF TOTAL"
90  PRINT
100 FOR I = 1 TO 5
110 PRINT I; P(I); INT (0.5 + 100 * P(I)/T)
120 NEXT I
```

In this example P is the array variable. In general naming conventions for numeric array variables are the same as those for ordinary numeric variables.

(b) String arrays

Just as it is useful to have numeric arrays so it can be useful to employ string arrays. String-array variables are formed in a similar way to numeric-array variables, by placing a label after a normal variable name e.g. D$(5). As an example of their use let's improve our last program by adding these lines,

    11 A$ = "MONTUEWEDTHUFRI"
    12 FOR I = 1 TO 5
    13 D$(I) = MID$(A$, 3*I − 2, 3)
    14 NEXT I

and changing line 110 into

    110 PRINT D$(I); P(I); INT(0.5 + 100*P(I)/T)

The effect of these changes will be to replace the day number in the output display into the appropriate three character abbreviation for the day name.

(c) The DIMENSION statement

In the examples of arrays we have seen so far, no array has had a label of 10 or higher. If arrays of 10 or more elements are to be used then a DIMENSION statement is required, e.g.

    10 DIM N(20), A$(15)

will set up the array N with 20 elements and A$ with 15 elements. The maximum number of array elements that can be used depends on the machine. Usually DIMENSION statements are placed at the beginning of a program, and more than one statement can be used if required. As a final point about numeric arrays at this stage, it should be noted that tables of numbers can be referred to by two-dimensional arrays, so that N(3,5), say, could refer to the number in the third row and fifth column of the table, however we will not pursue this concept further here.

6.2 The READ and DATA statements

READ and DATA statement types are used to store data in a program, and to read them into an appropriate variable when required. For example,

    10 FOR I = 1 TO 5
    20 READ N
    25 PRINT N
    30 NEXT I
    40 DATA 5,23,17,199,3

will succesively read the values 5,23,17,199 and 3 into the variable N, printing the value out each time. String variables can be handled as well, as the following example shows. This calculates the utilisation of four types of equipment, from an input of the hours for which they have been used out of an assumed maximum of 50 hours.

```
10  FOR I = 1 TO 4
20  READ E$(I)
30  PRINT "INPUT HOURS THAT " E$(I) " EQUIP-
    MENT HAS BEEN USED"
40  INPUT U(I)
50  NEXT I
60  PRINT
70  PRINT "EQUIPMENT UTILISATION SUMMARY"
80  PRINT
90  PRINT "EQUIPMENT  HRS USED  %UTILISATION"
100 FOR I = 1 TO 4
110 PRINT E$(I); U(I); 100*U(I)/50
120 NEXT I
130 DATA GRINDING, MILLING, TURNING, WELDING
```

Numeric and string data can be used together in DATA statements (several statements can be used if required), and the computer will always keep track of which item is to be read next. If you wish reading to recommence from the first DATA statement in the program then a RESTORE statement can be used, e.g.

500 RESTORE

The effect of this statement when encountered during the processing of a program will be to reset the computer's 'pointer' so that the next READ statement starts reading the data from the first DATA statement in the program.

The main area of application for READ and DATA statements is in the storage and retrieval of relatively small amounts of data, say up to five fields of data for each of fifty items. In Chapter 9 we shall consider a file management program based on READ and DATA statements. The main disadvantage of using these statements lies in the fact that making changes to the data requires the program to be changed and the new version to be stored, as opposed to a system using disk or tape storage in which files of information are updated but the program remains unchanged. The advantage of using READ and DATA is that they are simpler to use than file-input and file-output statements which are beyond the scope of this book.

6.3 Subroutines

(a) The GOSUB and RETURN statements

Occasionally when you are writing a program the need arises to use the same statements at two or more different points in the program. Such groups of statements can be handled as subroutines, and in BASIC they are called for by using the GOSUB statement. Processing continues from the line following the GOSUB statement after the subroutine statements have been executed and when a RETURN statement is encountered at the end of the subroutine. As an example consider the program below, which calculates the square root and cube root of a number, with a subroutine (lines 300–500) to cut down the numeric output to occupy exactly 5 characters.

```
10   PRINT "INPUT A NUMBER"
20   INPUT N
30   X = N ↑ 0.5
40   GOSUB 300
50   PRINT A$ " IS ITS SQUARE ROOT"
60   X = N ↑ (1/3)
70   GOSUB 300
80   PRINT A$ " IS ITS CUBE ROOT"
90   GOTO 600
300  A$ = STR$(X)
310  L = LEN(A$)
320  IF L = 5 THEN 500
330  IF L > 5 THEN 400
340  REM ***L < 5 IF PROCESSING GETS TO THIS POINT
350  FOR I = 1 TO (5 − L)
360  A$ = " " + A$
370  NEXT I
380  GOTO 500
400  A$ = MID$(A$, 1, 5)
500  RETURN
600  END
```

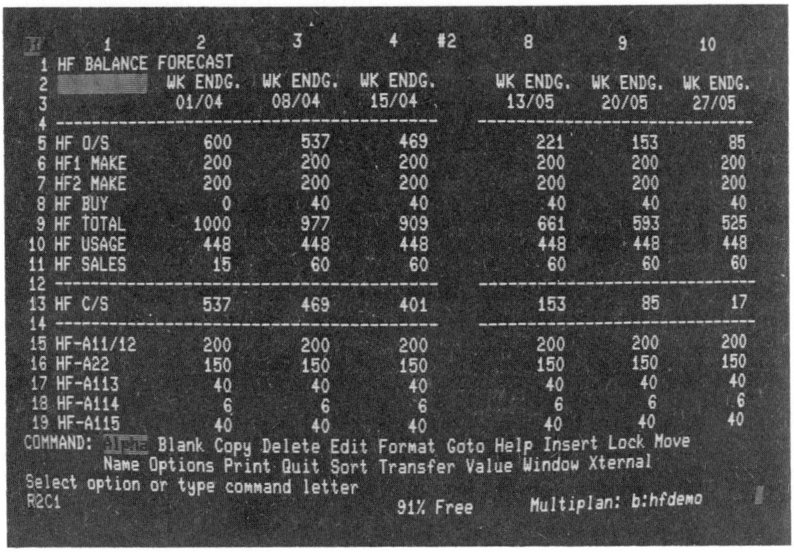

Fig. 6.1 An example of a spreadsheet screen.

Notice that this subroutine requires the variable X to have the value which is to be truncated if necessary, and that it returns the truncated string set up in the variable A$. Notice too that line 90 is required to avoid the program processing the subroutine a third and unwanted time. As many subroutines as are required may be used in a BASIC program, and for clarity they are usually best placed at the end of the main body of the program. As well as enabling lines of code to be used more than once subroutines do have another function in that they provide a good method of structuring a program into its logical components. This is a great aid to other programmers reading it, and also to the ease with which it may be changed should the need arise.

6.4 The GET statement

The GET statement instructs the computer to search for a single character of keyboard input and to assign it to a string variable. If no key depression is detected then the string variable has what is called the null string assigned to it, that is a string with no characters, represented by two quote characters with nothing between them (not even a space character). Processing therefore continues whether or not a key is depressed during the short time in which the keyboard is scanned. To overcome the synchronisation problem the following approach is usually adopted.

```
50 GET Z$
60 IF Z$ = "" THEN 50
```

Here the null string is detected by an IF statement which sends the program round in a loop until a key depression is detected, at which point processing will continue with the statement following line 60, Z$ having been set as the single character of the key that was depressed.

The GET statement is particularly useful for three main tasks.
  (i) Performing validity checks on data as it is keyed in character by character (e.g. detecting if letters are entered when numbers are required). The advantage over the INPUT statement is that appropriate actions can be written into the program to cater for errors, instead of a simple 'TYPE MISMATCH' error message being displayed.
  (ii) Enabling real-time interaction in simulations or games. Here the program will include a GET statement as part of a bigger loop. If a key depression is detected then some appropriate action will be taken (to alter the settings on some simulated piece of equipment, or to fire at the space invaders!), otherwise the simulation will proceed uninterrupted.

(iii) Allowing the whole of the display screen to be used to show a table or graph, until a key is pressed as a signal to change or replace the display.

6.5 System commands and cursor addressing

(a) System commands

System commands are those instructions which control the operation and storage of programs. They are typed directly from the keyboard and initiated by pressing the return or enter key. They differ in detail between different manufacturers' machines, but those given below for the Commodore PET are fairly typical.

Command	Function
RUN	Executes the program currently stored in RAM.
LOAD "program name"	Loads a named program from cassette tape deck into RAM.
SAVE "program name"	Saves (stores) a program currently in RAM onto a cassette tape under the given name.
NEW	Clears the existing program from RAM.

(b) Cursor addressing

The cursor is the name given to that character, which is usually a flashing square or dash, that signifies the position where the next screen character will be displayed. Cursor addressing is the facility, available on the PET and similar machines, which allows the display of characters to be made at any position on the screen. This is in contrast to the simple 'teletype' operation, in which output is restricted to lines of characters one after the other with a new line being automatically begun when the old line is full. Inevitably cursor addressing methods vary considerably between different machines. The method shown in Table 6.1 is applicable to the Commodore PET and VIC machines, and is based on the use of the familiar PRINT statement. Essentially the Commodore PRINT statement allows the following special keys to be stored as 'characters' within the quotation marks of a text string. To employ cursor addressing simply press any of the above keys within the quotation marks of a PRINT statement. For example

10 PRINT " ⌑ A HEADING"

when run will result in the screen being cleared and the title 'A HEADING' being printed at the top left hand corner. (The heart

Key	Mode	Function	Symbol
CLR HOME	NORMAL	Moves the cursor 'home' to the top left-hand corner of the screen, without affecting the existing screen display.	
CLR HOME	SHIFT	Clears the screen completely and also moves the cursor (home) to the top left-hand corner.	
CRSR	NORMAL	Moves the cursor down one line.	
CRSR	SHIFT	Moves the cursor up one line.	
CRSR	NORMAL	Moves the cursor one character to the right.	
CRSR	SHIFT	Moves the cursor one character to the left.	

Table 6.1

character is what appears in a print statement when SHIFT CLR HOME is pressed. Similarly the cursor up, down, left and right characters each have their own special symbol, and result in the display position moving appropriately.) Note that after any PRINT statement using cursor addressing a straightforward PRINT statement without cursor addressing will begin printing at the left-hand side of the line immediately below the last cursor position.

Exercises 6

1 Write a program which requires ten numbers to be keyed in, assigns them to an array, and then identifies and displays the group of three consecutive numbers which have the highest total. (This procedure might be used in calculating an individual's pensionable salary where the numbers relate to salaries in the last ten years of work, or it might be of interest in a manufacturing process where the numbers relate to the values of a particular dimension of a batch of ten components being produced.)

2 Write a program which will hold in DATA statements:
  (i) a number, representing the number of months production totals that are held in subsequent DATA statements;
  (ii) a production total for each of the months.

The program should read the DATA statements and produce an output table similar to that shown on page 64, using a string array to print the abbreviated month names.

Month	Production	Cumulative Total to date
JAN	1510	1510
FEB	1316	2826
MAR	1629	4455
etc.		

3 Write a program that requests 15 pairs of length and diameter readings to be keyed in, which calculates and displays the average length and diameter, and which uses a subroutine which rejects data outside of the following ranges, asking for fresh values as soon as an invalid one is rejected.

   Valid length range   10.1 to 10.6 cm.
   Valid diameter range   3 to 7 mm.

4 Write a program which accepts as input 10 numbers between 0 and 100, and for each number produces a line of asterisks, the length of which is proportional to its value, with a value of 100 being taken as occupying 25 columns. (Hint: make use of a string consisting of 25 asterisks.)

5 Write a program which requests as input ten pairs of names and scores, and which displays as output the names and values of the highest and lowest scorers. If the highest or lowest scores are not the only ones with these values print a message which says this, but do not attempt to explicitly show each tied scorer.

6 Write a program which will display a question and a multiple choice of three answers A, B or C. Use a GET statement to accept the user's choice of A, B or C (rejecting any invalid responses) and to display an appropriate screen of information for the choice selected.

7 Program Flowcharts and Documentation

7.1 The use of program flowcharts

A program flowchart is a diagram which uses standard symbols with some annotation to illustrate the logic of a program. As such it serves two main functions:
  (i) it can be a useful first step towards creating the program language statements, i.e. it enables the logic to be set down and the writing of the program to be treated as a secondary step involving the 'translation' of the logical steps into program language statements;
  (ii) it forms a valuable item of program documentation, enabling the logical processes of the program to be viewed and understood without the distracting detail of a full program listing.

Program flowcharts are widely used to achieve both of the functions mentioned above. However in the author's experience few students, and even fewer technical programmers, use flowcharting as the first step in program writing (function (i)). Very often it is the description of what the program does which is achieved, by drawing up the flowchart after the coding of program statements is complete (function (ii)). Some of the reasons for this are given below.
  (i) For simple programs or programs which closely follow some mathematical procedure, it is easier to write the program statements down directly than it is to go through the extra flowcharting stage. (Screen editing facilities which are now standard on most microcomputers have contributed to this.)
  (ii) Making changes or corrections to a flowchart often results in the need for a complete re-draft.
  (iii) Students grappling with the construction and rules of a new language find it difficult to isolate and comprehend the process of flowcharting. (The immediacy of microcomputer access makes it difficult to ensure that students understand flowcharting before they use the machine.)
  (iv) The BASIC FOR . . . NEXT loop, which has its counterparts in other high-level languages, cannot be represented concisely with the standard flowchart symbols. In

other words if the flowchart is drawn up to be independent of the programming language, then it will include adding 1 to the loop counter and testing its value, which the BASIC language hides from the programmer. Nevertheless flowcharts can be a very helpful aid when one is faced with a complex logical problem to be programmed, and the need for an understanding of them so that documentation describing what the program does can be completed and understood by others, warrant that they be given serious attention.

7.2 Standard program flowcharting symbols

The standard program flowcharting symbols are listed in Table 7.1.

Table 7.1

Symbol	Logical step represented
parallelogram	An operation involving the input or output of data.
rectangle	A calculation or manipulation of data.
diamond	A decision.
rounded rectangle	A terminal, representing either the start or end of the program.
arrow	A flowline, indicating the sequence in which operations are to be performed.
→(3)	An off-page connector, used to show the continuation of the logical sequence onto another page of the flowchart.

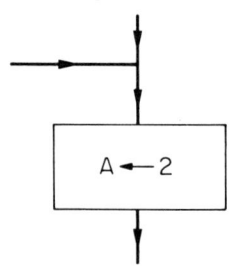

There are some useful conventions which help to make flowcharts easy to follow. They are shown on the left.

(i) It is useful if symbols have only one entering flowline, which means that flowline junctions may be required.

(ii) Wherever possible the flowlines should pass from the top of the page to the bottom, and hence from the bottom of one symbol to the top of the next. In particular the decision symbol may have two or three flowlines coming out of it, and each of these should be clearly labelled with the decision they represent, e.g. YES, NO or $>$, $<$, $=$.

(iii) Assignment of a value to a variable should be indicated as shown in the example on the left.

7.3 A simple example

The flowchart in Figure 7.1 represents the BASIC program to convert Centigrade temperatures to Fahrenheit which is listed in Section 4.5, with the additional statements 42–48 of Section 4.8.

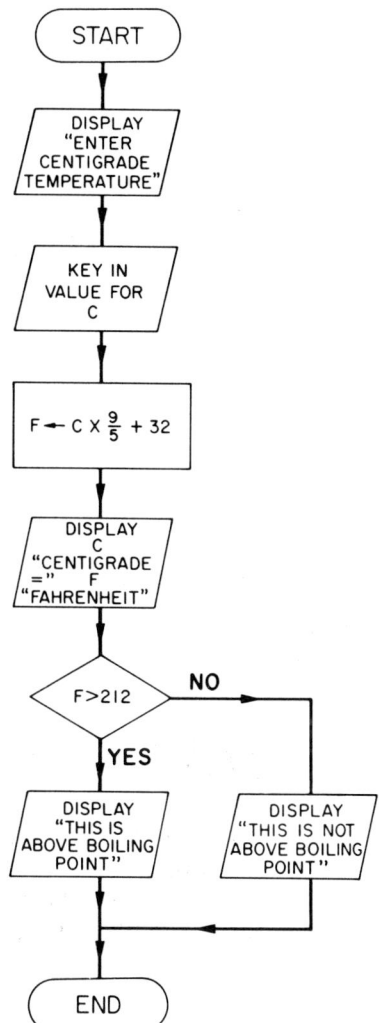

Fig. 7.1 The flowchart for the program to convert degrees Centigrade to degrees Fahrenheit.

7.4 Another example

The flowchart of Figure 7.2 represents the logic of a program to answer question 3 of Exercises 4, which uses Newton's Method to calculate a cube root. Note the use of the modulus, or absolute value, of the difference $Y - X$ to test if the program should be terminated, and the iterative loop in which the value of Y is given to X.

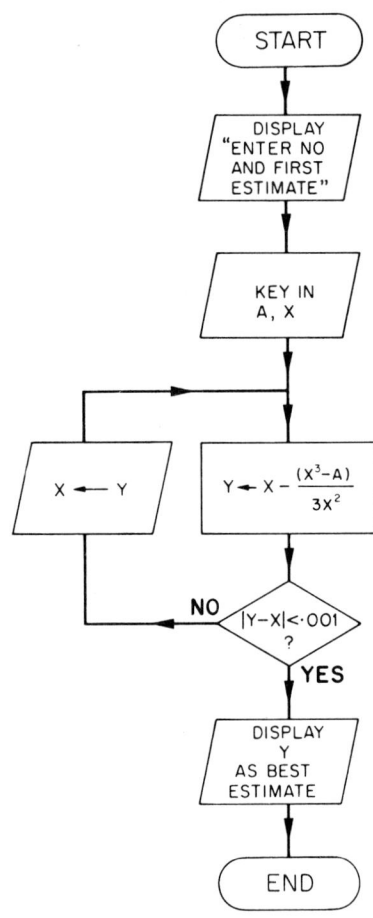

Fig. 7.2 The flowchart for the program to find a cube root using Newton's Method.

7.5 Building up a flowchart

As an illustration of the processes involved in building up a flowchart consider the problem of calculating the roots of a quadratic equation of the form $AX^2 + BX + C = 0$. The expression for calculating the roots is

$$\frac{-B \pm \sqrt{B^2 - 4AC}}{2A}$$

and there are three possible situations which may occur.
    (i) $B^2 - 4AC > 0$, giving two real roots.
   (ii) $B^2 - 4AC = 0$, giving one real double root.
  (iii) $B^2 - 4AC < 0$, giving no real roots.

In writing a flowchart for a program to handle the input of values for A, B and C and the subsequent display of the corresponding roots, the value of the expression $B^2 - 4AC$ will clearly play a central role. Consequently we would start our flowchart as shown in Figure 7.3, with the value of this

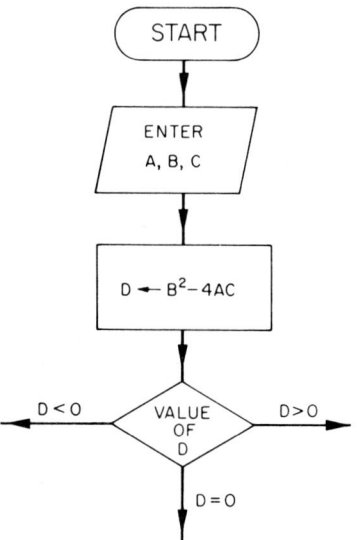

Fig. 7.3 A flowchart showing the first stage in solving quadratic equations.

expression being evaluated at an early stage so as to influence the logic paths which are being developed.

Having got this sound foundation we can now proceed to put the flesh on each of the three branches from the decision diamond as shown in Figure 7.4. In this example, once the

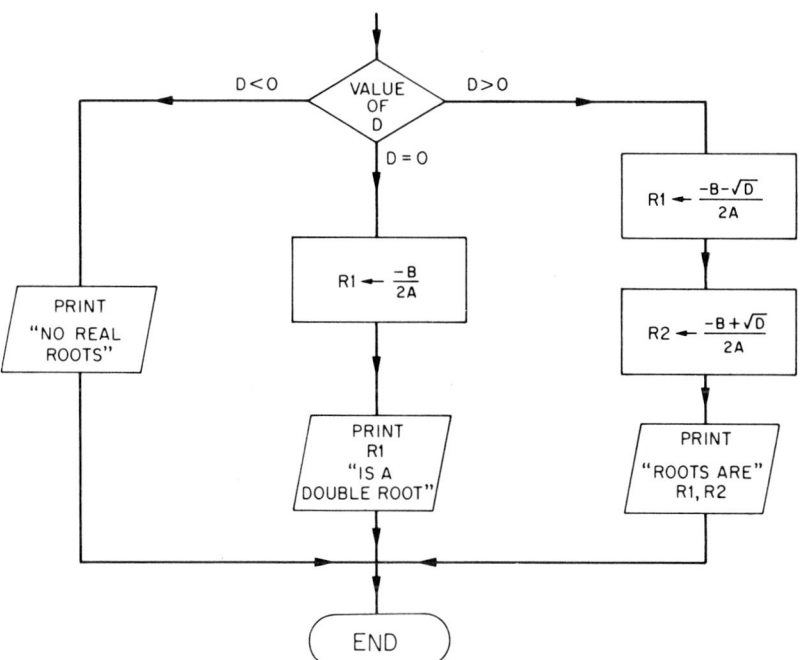

Fig. 7.4 A flowchart showing the second stage in solving quadratic equations.

foundation has been laid, the logic is straightforward enough for the first draft of the flowchart to be perfectly satisfactory. In more complex situations at least a third draft is normally required before the flowchart is in its final form. The next example illustrates this point.

7.6 A more complicated flowchart —the bubble sort

A procedure for sorting a list of numbers into ascending order can be summarised by the outline flowchart shown in Figure 7.5. For

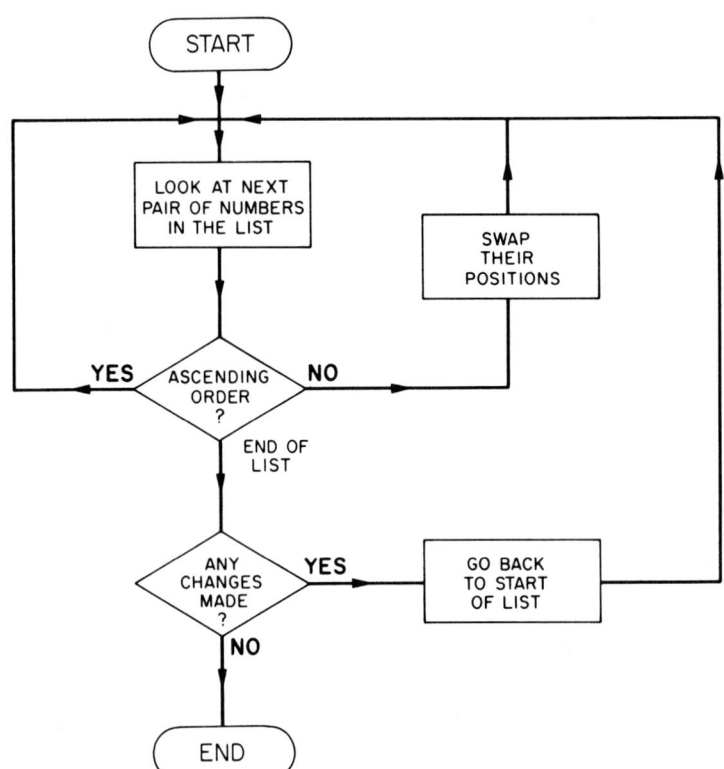

Fig. 7.5 An outline flowchart for a bubble-sort program.

example, if this procedure is applied to the list of numbers 7, 5, 9, 3 then the list will be transformed as shown in Table 7.2. Because of the way in which low numbers float to the front of the list this is known as a bubble sort.

As a first draft our outline flowchart is useful, but to provide a useful basis for programming we might produce the second draft (Figure 7.6), using an array L(I) to represent the list of N numbers.

This second draft lacks detail about the method of detecting if

Program Flowcharts and Documentation 71

Table 7.2

	Ascending order?	*Swap to:*
First pass		
7, 5, 9, 3	no	5, 7, 9, 3
5, **7, 9**, 3	yes	
5, 7, **9, 3**	no	5, 7, 3, 9
Second pass		
5, 7, 3, 9	yes	
5, **7, 3**, 9	no	5, 3, 7, 9
5, 3, **7, 9**	yes	
Third pass		
5, 3, 7, 9	no	3, 5, 7, 9
3, **5, 7**, 9	yes	
3, 5, **7, 9**	yes	
Fourth pass		
3, 5, 7, 9	yes	
3, **5, 7**, 9	yes	
3, 5, **7, 9**	yes	
	No changes so procedure is complete	

any changes have been made in each pass, and a third and final draft is required as shown in Figure 7.7.

The practice of arriving at a final version of a flowchart after several drafts is a common one, with the early drafts often being embellished with crossings out and inserts. If we examine the process by which the final draft was developed a little more closely, we see that once the idea of using an array was pursued in the second draft then the introduction of the position indicator, I, followed. The initial value of zero for I, the position of the test for I being less than N-1, and the point at which the indicator was incremented by one were all chosen somewhat intuitively with a trial and error technique to see if the choices made would have the desired effect. The last feature to be introduced was the counter, C, which was included in the third draft to keep track of whether or not any changes have been made during a particular pass through the list. It is an important feature because this is the factor which eventually terminates the program when no swaps have been required. Note that this flowchart does not deal with

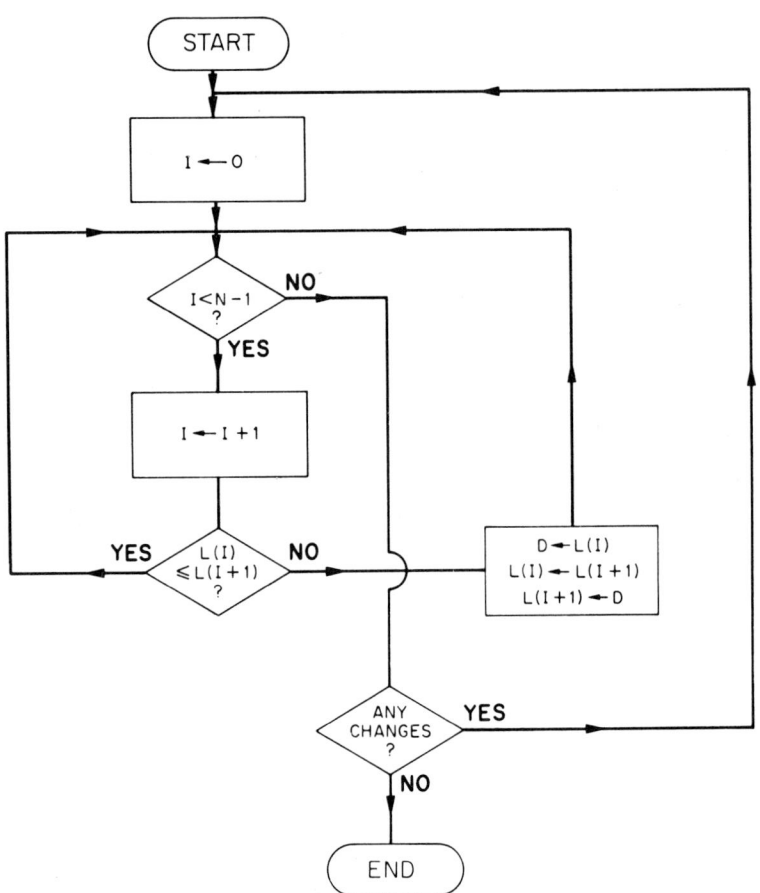

Fig. 7.6 A second draft of the flowchart for a bubble-sort program.

the logic for reading in values for N and the list of numbers L(I), nor does it deal with any actions to be taken with the list in its sorted form.

7.7 Program documentation

There are five categories of documentation which are used to record the details of a program, and it is good practice to employ each category in a commercial or industrial application where the program maintenance is likely to be handed on when staff changes occur. The prime function of documentation is to enable the program to be understood easily by anyone who may later have an interest in it (including its author!), enabling its results to be interpreted correctly and modifications to be made efficiently.

(a) Program description/specification

Depending on the size and nature of the program this category includes:

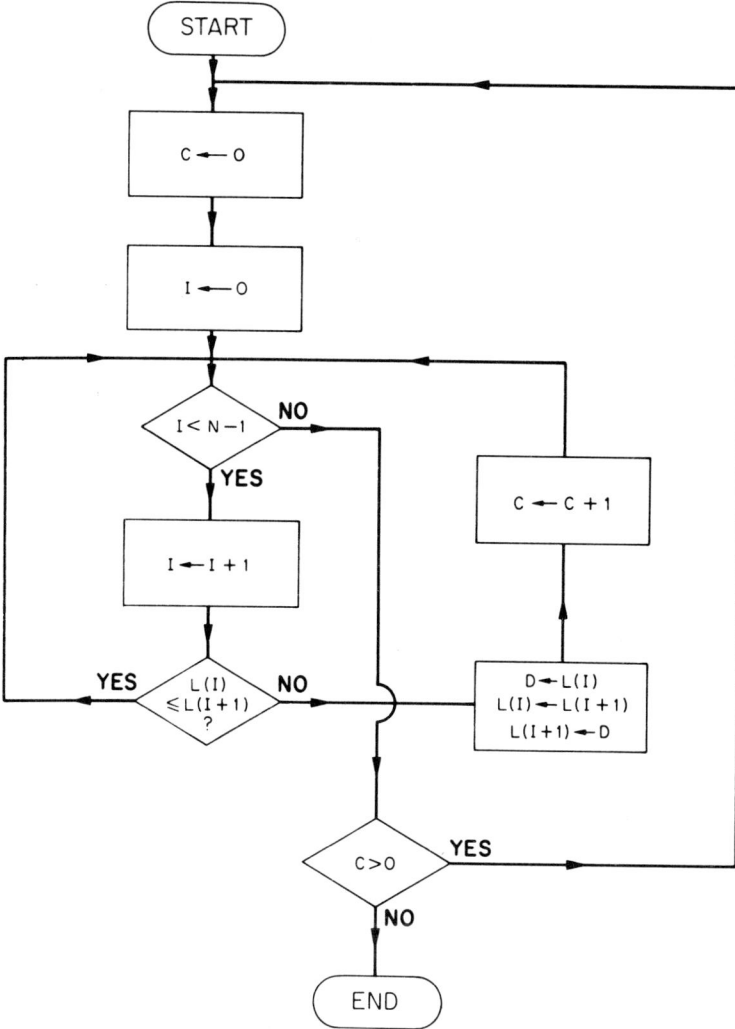

Fig. 7.7 The final flowchart for a bubble-sort program.

(i) an outline description, without computer jargon, of what the program is to achieve in broad terms;
(ii) a detailed specification of the tasks to be performed, and the methods to be employed to achieve them;
(iii) a guide to a user of the system, enabling the input data to be assembled and given to the computer in the correct format, the program to be run successfully, and the results to be clearly understood.

(b) A program listing

A hard-copy printout of a program is an obvious and essential item, and it is much more useful if it is liberally sprinkled with appropriate comment statements (such as REMARK statements in BASIC).

(c) A flowchart

As stated in Section 7.1 a flowchart forms an important part of a program's documentation, and is one of the parts which those who did not write the program find easiest to understand.

(d) A variable list

This is a list of all the variables used in the program and their significance. If the list is a long one then keeping it in alphabetical

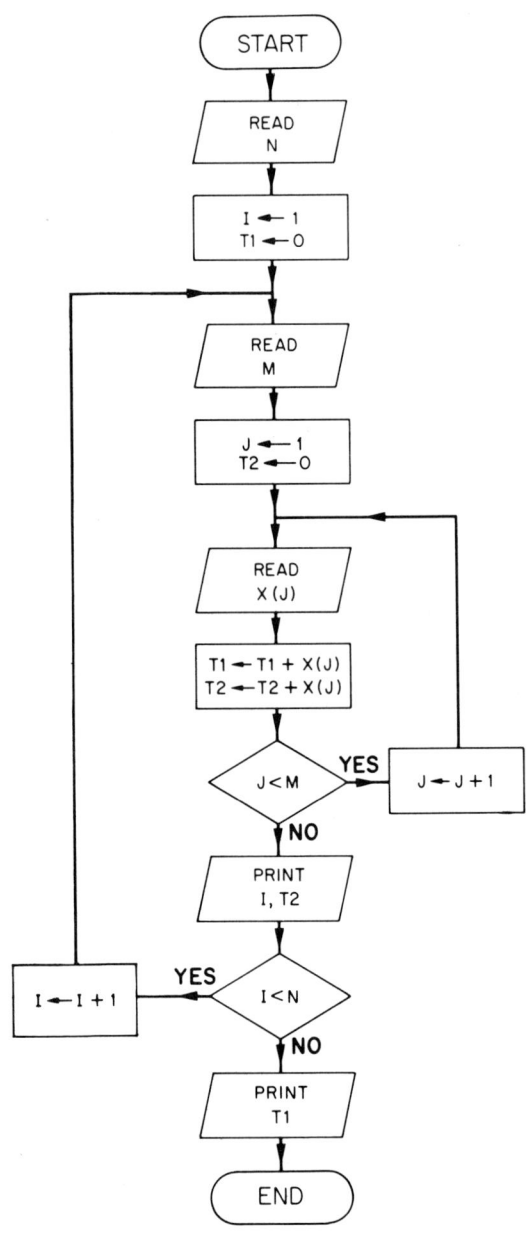

Fig. 7.8 A flowchart for the bubble-sort program used in Exercises 7, question 5.

order will be more beneficial than grouping together variables with similar functions or areas of use.

(e) Test data and results

A vital part of program development is the use of some test data with the program, and the comparison of the actual results with those expected. An obvious point, but one which needs to be stressed, is that the expected results of test data should be determined before the actual results are examined. The act of calculating the expected results can often bring to light logical steps that were overlooked in the original program design. Test data and results, suitably annotated, should be kept to provide a further means of ensuring that a newcomer understands the program. They may also prove useful in the event of operational difficulties.

Exercises 7

1 Write a flowchart for making tea for two, starting from the diagram on the left.
2 Write a flowchart for a program to take as input the number of numbers in a list and the numbers themselves. The program should sort the list into descending order, each number that is output being accompanied by its position in the sorted list (i.e. 1, 2, 3 . . . etc.).
3 Write a flowchart for the program in question 5 of Exercises 5, with the additional feature that a safe landing is judged to have taken place if the height is between 0 and 30 m and the speed of fall is less than 10 ms^{-1}.
4 Write a detailed flowchart for the program in question 1 of Exercises 6.
5 List the outputs that would be displayed from the program represented by the flowchart of Figure 7.8, assuming that the data input were as follows:

   3, 2, 9, 7, 3, 4, 1, 8, 1, 5

6 Describe the advantages of using program flowcharts, and explain what is meant by program documentation.

8 A Graph-Plotting Program

8.1 Outline

This chapter is devoted to the consideration of a graph-plotting program, including a full program listing and explanation, a flowchart and illustrations of the program's output. The program merits attention because it provides a general purpose plotting facility, useful over a broad spectrum of technical applications, and achieves this in only 30 statements without the use of arrays. The program does make use of the Commodore PET's cursor addressing facilities, but these are paralleled on most microcomputer systems. A special feature of the program is a facility to change the horizontal and vertical scales of the graph, so that the superficially limited resolution of the screen can be overcome by simply homing in on a particular region of the graph which is of interest.

8.2 Theory

The only piece of mathematical theory on which this program is based concerns the relationships between X and Y values on either side of a curve which is to be plotted. For example consider Figure 8.1.

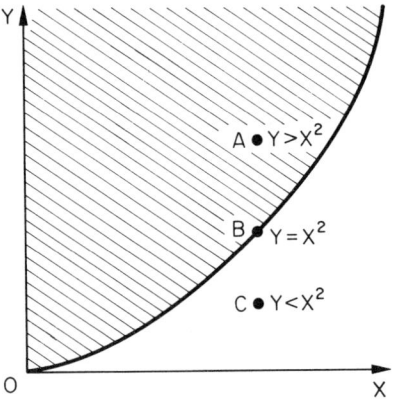

Fig. 8.1 A graph of $Y = X^2$.

A Graph-Plotting Program 77

The curve on which point B lies is made up of points at which $Y = X^2$. At points like A (which are vertically above B) Y is greater than X^2 since their Y value is greater than that of B, while at points like C (which are vertically below B) Y is less than X^2 since their Y value is less than that of B. The difference is emphasised in Figure 8.1 by shading the area in which Y is greater than X^2. The program uses this bit of theory to print shaded characters where $Y > X^2$ and brighter characters where $Y < X^2$. Using this method there is no need to plot the curve $Y = X^2$, it is simply a matter of

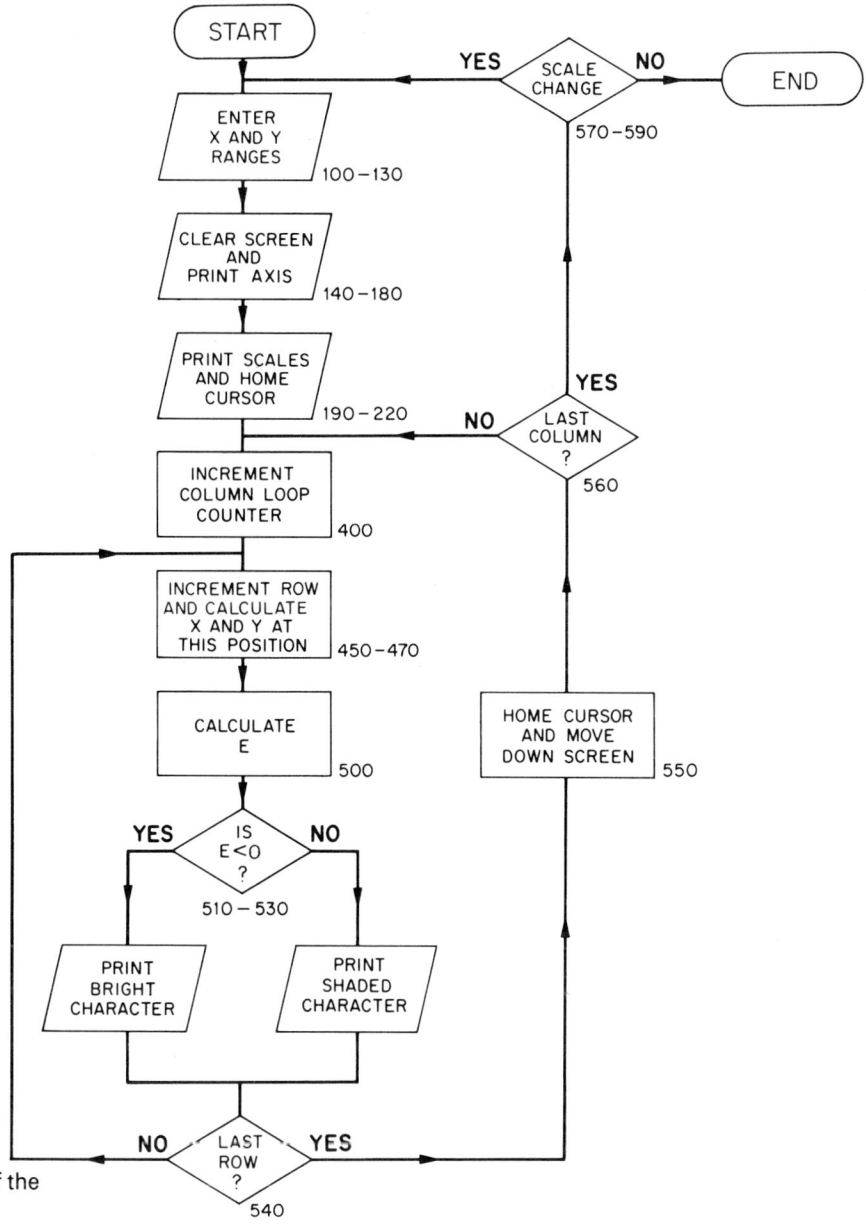

Fig. 8.2 The flowchart of the graph-plotting program.

displaying the right shading in each character position on the graph and the curve emerges as the boundary between the differently-shaded regions. This boundary naturally appears stepped due to the limited number of characters on the screen (21 rows of 21 columns are used for the graph) but any degree of accuracy within the arithmetic limits of the computer can be achieved by changing the scales so that the whole graph is used to plot what was just a small part of the previous screen.

The graph to be plotted is defined in line 500 of the program, where an expression E is evaluated. Later it is tested to see if it is positive or negative. For example we have

$$500 \; E = Y - X \uparrow 2 \qquad \text{to plot } Y = X^2$$

and we can easily change this to

$$500 \; E = Y - 3 * X - 2 \qquad \text{to plot } Y = 3X + 2$$

More sophisticated expressions can easily be inserted in line 500 at any time after the program is loaded, simply by typing a new line 500 and then pressing the return key.

8.3 A flowchart of the program

Figure 8.2 gives a program flowchart which illustrates the logic of the program, the numbers refer to the relevant program statement numbers.

8.4 Explanation of the program listing

Figure 8.3 is a listing of the statements which make up the program, and an explanation of each part of the logic is given below.

Line(s)	Comments
50	This remark statement gives the program's title and explains that line 500 can be changed to plot a different curve.
100–110	These ask for, and receive, the minimum and maximum values of Y in the chosen range: YI holds the minimum value, YA holds the maximum value.
120–130	Ditto for the range of values of X.
140	This PRINT statement uses a cursor addressing instruction within its quotes. The character is obtained by pressing the SHIFT and CLEAR

```
50 REM**** GRAPH PLOTTING PROGRAM ***** CHANGE LINE 500 TO PLOT DIFFERENT CURVE
100 PRINT"⌂ENTER Y RANGE (MIN,MAX)"
110 INPUT YI,YA
120 PRINT"ENTER X RANGE (MIN,MAX)"
130 INPUT XI,XA
140 PRINT"⌂"
150 FOR K=1 TO 21
160 PRINT TAB(11)"⊣"
170 NEXT K
180 PRINT"              └┬┬┬┬┬┬┬┬┬┬┬┬┬┬┬┬┬┬┬┬┬┘"
190 PRINT TAB(11)XITAB(21)(XI+XA)/2TAB(31)XA
200 PRINT"⌂▮"YA
210 PRINT"▮▮▮▮▮▮▮▮▮▮"(YA+YI)/2
220 PRINT"▮▮▮▮▮▮▮▮▮▮"YI"⌂"
400 FOR I=1 TO 21
450 FOR J=1 TO 21
460 X=XI+((I-1)/20*(XA-XI))
470 Y=YI+((J-1)/20*(YA-YI))
500 E=Y-X↑2
510 B$="▮"
520 IF E<0 THEN B$="▮ ▮"
530 PRINT TAB(11+I)B$
535 PRINT"⌂⌂⌂"
540 NEXT J
550 PRINT"▮▮▮▮▮▮▮▮▮▮▮▮▮▮▮▮▮▮▮▮▮"
560 NEXT I
570 PRINT"▮▮▮SCALE CHANGE (Y OR N)";
580 INPUT Q$
590 IF Q$="Y" THEN 100
1000 END
READY.
```

Fig. 8.3 The program listing for the graph-plotting program.

	HOME keys together after the first quotes. The effect of this statement is to clear the screen and home the cursor at the top left hand corner of the screen.
150–170	This FOR.... NEXT loop prints the vertical Y-axis scale.
180	This prints the horizontal X-axis scale.
190	This prints the maximum, minimum and mid-point values of X under the X-axis.
200	This homes the cursor (without clearing the screen), moves it down a line and then prints the maximum value of Y beside the top of the Y-axis.
210	This moves the cursor to the middle of the Y axis and displays the mid-point value of Y beside it.
220	This displays the minimum value of Y alongside the bottom of the Y scale, and then moves the cursor up a line so that the next PRINT statement will print on the lowest row of the graph. (Without this the next PRINT statement would have printed one line further down the screen.)

400 This is the start of the loop for controlling the printing of a column. (The graph is made up of 21 columns.)

450 This is the start of the loop for controlling the printing of one character in one row of the current column. (The graph is made up of 21 rows.)

460 This calculates the appropriate value for X in the current column position I, from the formula
$$X = XI + \frac{(I-1)}{20} \times (XA - XI)$$
i.e. X = minimum value of X + (I − 1) twentieths of the range of X values.

470 This calculates the appropriate value for Y in the current row position J, from the formula
$$Y = YI + \frac{(J-1)}{20} \times (YA - YI)$$
i.e. Y = miminum value of Y + (J − 1) twentieths of the range of Y values.

500 This gives the value of the expression relating X and Y. In general to plot the curve Y = f(X), line 500 should read
$$500\ E = Y - f(X)$$

510 This sets the character to be printed as a shaded character (this may be overwritten in 520).

520 This changes the character to be printed to a bright character (a reverse field blank) if E < 0. Reverse field is obtained by pressing the RVS key within the quotes, it is switched off by pressing SHIFT and RVS before the quotes are closed, this accounts for the two strange characters within the quotes of this statement.

530 This displays the desired character in the correct position by using the TAB function to get to the correct column of the current row.

535 This moves the cursor up three spaces so as to prepare for displaying the next character one row higher up.

540 This ends the row loop which began at line 450.

550 This homes the cursor then moves it to the bottom row of the graph ready for the next column to be dealt with.

560 This ends the column loop which began at line

	400.
570-590	Asks if a new display with changed scales is required, and repeats from statement 100 if it is.
1000	This ends the program.

The statement numbering scheme may seem a little quaint, but it has been left as it appeared when the program was developed to illustrate the leaps in sequence that a programmer should build in to allow for the evolution of the program at the development stage: If a convenient renumbering process is available then it should be used when development is complete, but note that statement numbering can be used effectively to highlight logically related statements.

8.5 Results and test data

(a) The relationship $Y = X^2$

To plot the curve defined by the relationship $Y = X^2$ we write line 500 as

$$500 \; E = Y - X \uparrow 2$$

Before running the program with test data we must have an idea of what range of values we are going to consider, and what we expect the results to look like. In this example these steps are very simple, and we expect the curve shape seen in Figure 8.1 which is known as a parabola. Now because negative values of X when squared still give a positive value for Y, we may choose the following ranges for one test run.

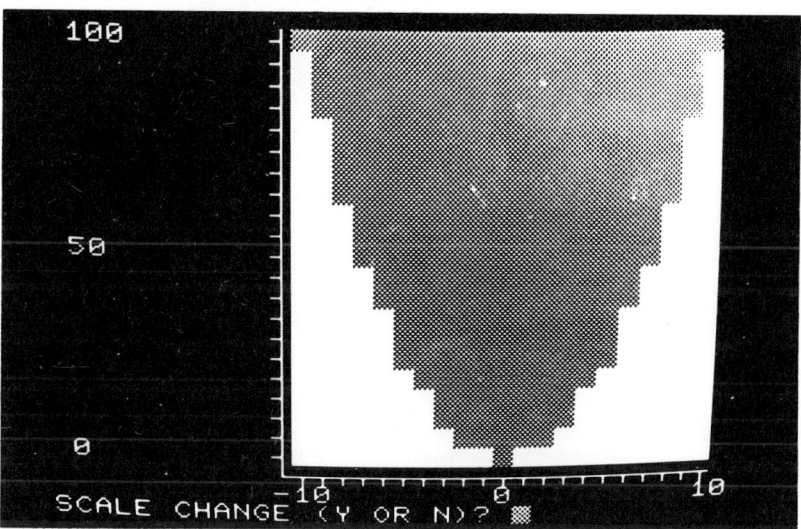

Fig. 8.4 A plot of the equation $Y = X^2$.

	minimum	maximum
Y	0	100
X	−10	10

We would expect the computer to produce the display which is illustrated in Figure 8.4. (Some comments on sorting out problems with the display format in a program like this are given in Section 8.5(c).) Although useful for confirming the shape of the curve, the resolution is insufficient for very accurate interpretation and a more useful display can be achieved by accepting a scale change and choosing the values

	minimum	maximum
Y	60	90
X	8	9

This produces the graph illustrated in Figure 8.5. At this point it is

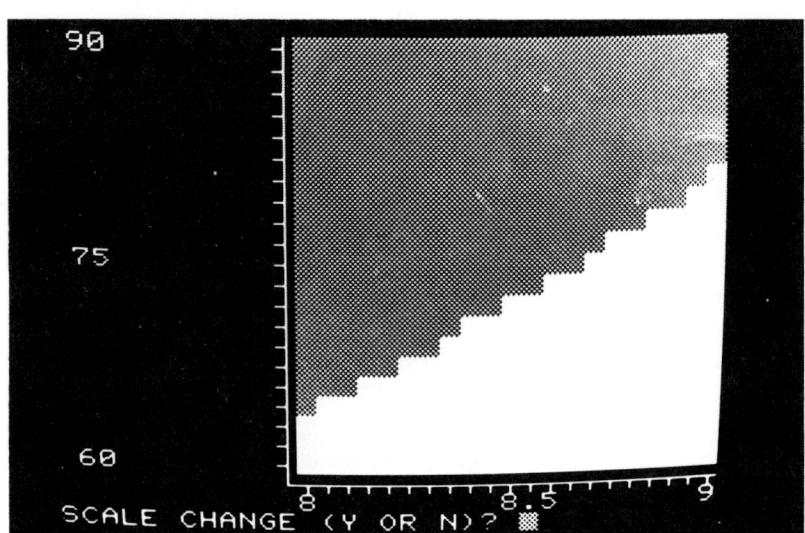

Fig. 8.5 A close-up of a region of Figure 8.4.

worth remarking that statement number 520 tests if E is less than zero, and it would have been just as logical for this statement to test if E is less than or equal to zero. This can affect (by one character) the position of the boundary between the two shaded regions. This is not critical however since the nature of the program invites the user to 'enlarge' the area of interest until the result is accurate enough.

(b) The relationship Y = COS X

This familiar trigonometric relationship can be plotted easily using the program, but one factor which has to be taken into account is the usual computer convention of expressing X in radians in a trigonometric function like COS(X). Since $180° = \pi$ radians the relationship becomes

$$Y = \text{COS} \frac{(X \times \pi)}{180}$$

where the units of X are taken to be degrees. Hence for line 500 we should have

500 E = Y − COS(π ∗ X/180)

(Note that π is an acceptable constant symbol which can be used directly on the PET, 3.1416 would be a suitable alternative.) We can use the range

	minimum	maximum
Y	−1	1
X	−360	360

which gives the curve shown in Figure 8.6. A consequence of line 520 for this curve is that the boundary is not seen to pass through the values of −1 and 1 for Y. Suitable scales for further investigation are

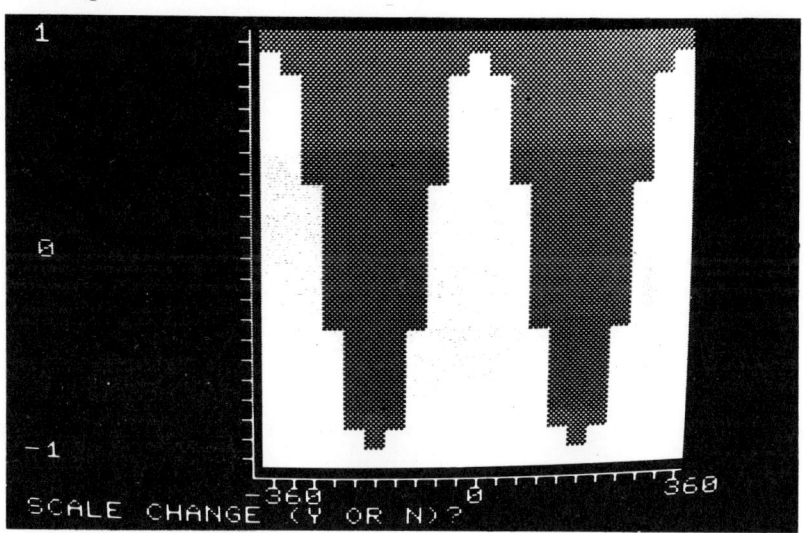

Fig. 8.6 A plot of the equation Y = COS X.

	minimum	maximum
Y	−1	1
X	−180	180

shown in Figure 8.7, and

	minimum	maximum
Y	0	0.2
X	80	90

shown in Figure 8.8.

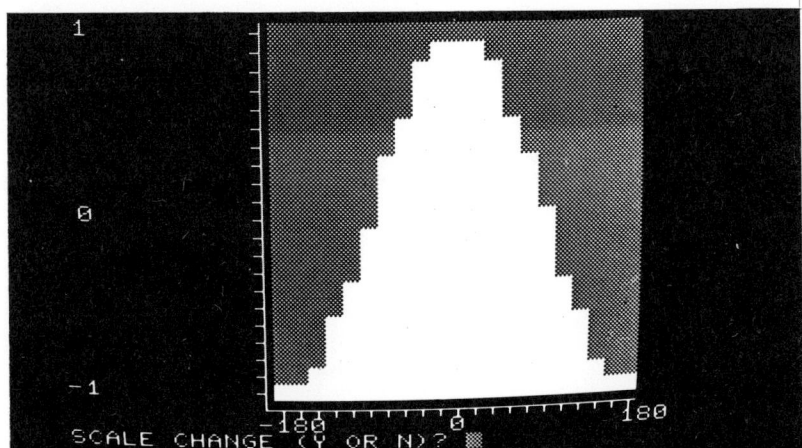

Fig. 8.7 A close-up of the central half of Figure 8.6.

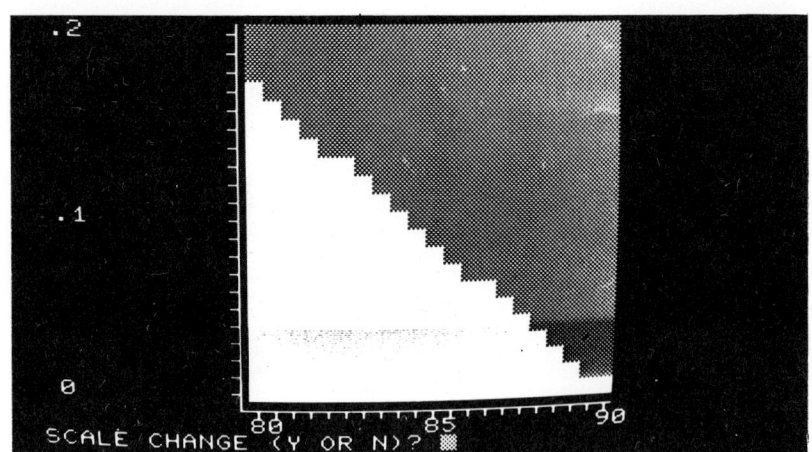

Fig. 8.8 A close-up of a small region of Figure 8.6.

(c) Comments on test data and testing

Section 7.7(c) emphasised the need to know what results to expect from test data before the actual output is examined, and clearly in the two examples above the expected results could be calculated or easily looked up in mathematical tables. The major and vital part of developing and testing a program like this, however, is getting used to using the graphic display. My advice here is that when it comes to deciding how many rows or columns to come down or go up in PRINT statements, it is wise to start with a figure derived from a relatively quick calculation. But be prepared to adjust that figure by trial and error, always being sure that you know why an adjustment has to be made before making it. This method of working would not have been suitable in the early days of computing when such programs would have to be run in batch mode. Homing the cursor from time to time (e.g. at the end of printing each column of the graph, as in line 550) can simplify the overall appearance of the logic since it is then clear which screen position the cursor is at in that particular part of the program.

Exercises 8

1 Use the plot program (Figure 8.3) to find the square root of 57, accurate to five decimal places.
2 Use the plot program to plot a polynomial of the form

$$Y = AX^4 + BX^3 + CX^2 + DX + K$$

where A, B, C, D and K are constants of your choice. Derive some test data and record the results of test runs.
3 Modify the plot program so that:
   (i) the mid-points of the Y and X axis scales are clearly marked on each scale with a '+';
   (ii) a title is printed on the graph showing the relationship that is being plotted. (You are allowed to put in PRINT statements with explicit titles.)
4 A break-even chart for the comparative costs of two alternative production processes looks like the one shown in Figure 8.9

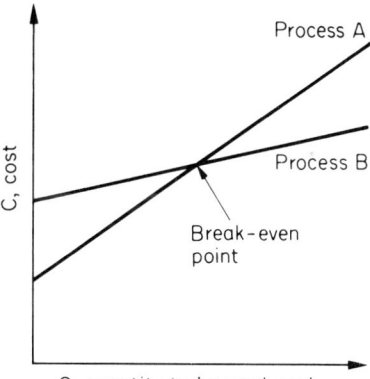

Fig. 8.9 A break-even chart to compare the production processes (A and B) which could be used to produce a product.

where each line is of the form $Y = V*Q + F$ where V is the variable cost per unit of production and F is a fixed cost including overheads for each process. Modify the plot program (using three shades instead of two) so that a break-even chart can be plotted.
5 Use the plot program to examine some mathematical/ technical/economic relationships that are of interest to you. Develop test data where possible.
6 What difference would it make if line 460 of the plot program (Figure 8.3) were placed instead as line 440? Are there any further improvements that could be made to the program?

A Data-Retrieval Program

9.1 Outline

In this chapter we will look at a program designed to enable several different kinds of question to be answered from one relatively small set of data. This particular program is concerned with information about the location and safety testing of large items of equipment. But the principles that it illustrates could equally well be applied to a wide variety of tasks where an item or individual has half a dozen or so details to be stored, and later retrieved. In contrast to the last program, which made much use of special PET features, this has been written in a form which should translate to other machines with very little effort. A consequence is that cosmetic features such as clearing the screen to begin a display from the top of the screen have been left out, and anyone writing a program derived from this one will be well advised to insert their own touches of screen layout design.

9.2 Program description

The program stores information in DATA statements (one per item of equipment) in the following categories.
- Registered number—a four digit number by which the equipment is uniquely identified.
- Equipment type—a text string description of what kind of equipment it is.
- Location—a text string description of where the equipment is usually located (the alphabetic characters have been preceded by full stops in the DATA statements as a simple way of aligning output).
- Test frequency—a number representing the number of months between regular safety tests.
- Month and year last tested—a number from 1 to 12 representing the month in which the equipment was last tested, and a two digit number corresponding to the year in which the last test took place.

The program is capable of answering four different types of question relating to this information as summarised below.

(i) Given a particular registered number it will display the details of the corresponding item of equipment, or display a message saying that it cannot be found.

(ii) Given a particular type of equipment it will display details of all items of that type.

(iii) Given the current year and month, it will display details of all equipment for which the next test is overdue.

(iv) Given the current year and month, it will display details of all equipment for which the next test is due within the next three months.

It is assumed that the DATA statements will be amended when items are actually tested, or added to, or deleted from the firm's list of assets. Clearly this method of storing data is only effective for small databases (up to a hundred or so items say) where changes do not have to be made very often. Alternative methods would involve the use of magnetic-tape or disk files, the principles of which are discussed in earlier chapters.

9.3 Program flowchart

Figure 9.1 is an outline flowchart of the logic of the data retrieval program.

9.4 Program listing and explanation

The program listing is given in Figure 9.2 and comments on the program follow.

Line(s)	Comments
50	This reads the number of items for which data are stored. The corresponding DATA statement is line 1000 which would have to be changed if there was any increase or decrease in the number of items recorded.
100–230	These display the 'menu' of options which a user of the program may choose from and jump to the relevant statements. Note that line 220 is a validity check rejecting input which does not fall into the four options offered.

88 Use of Computers

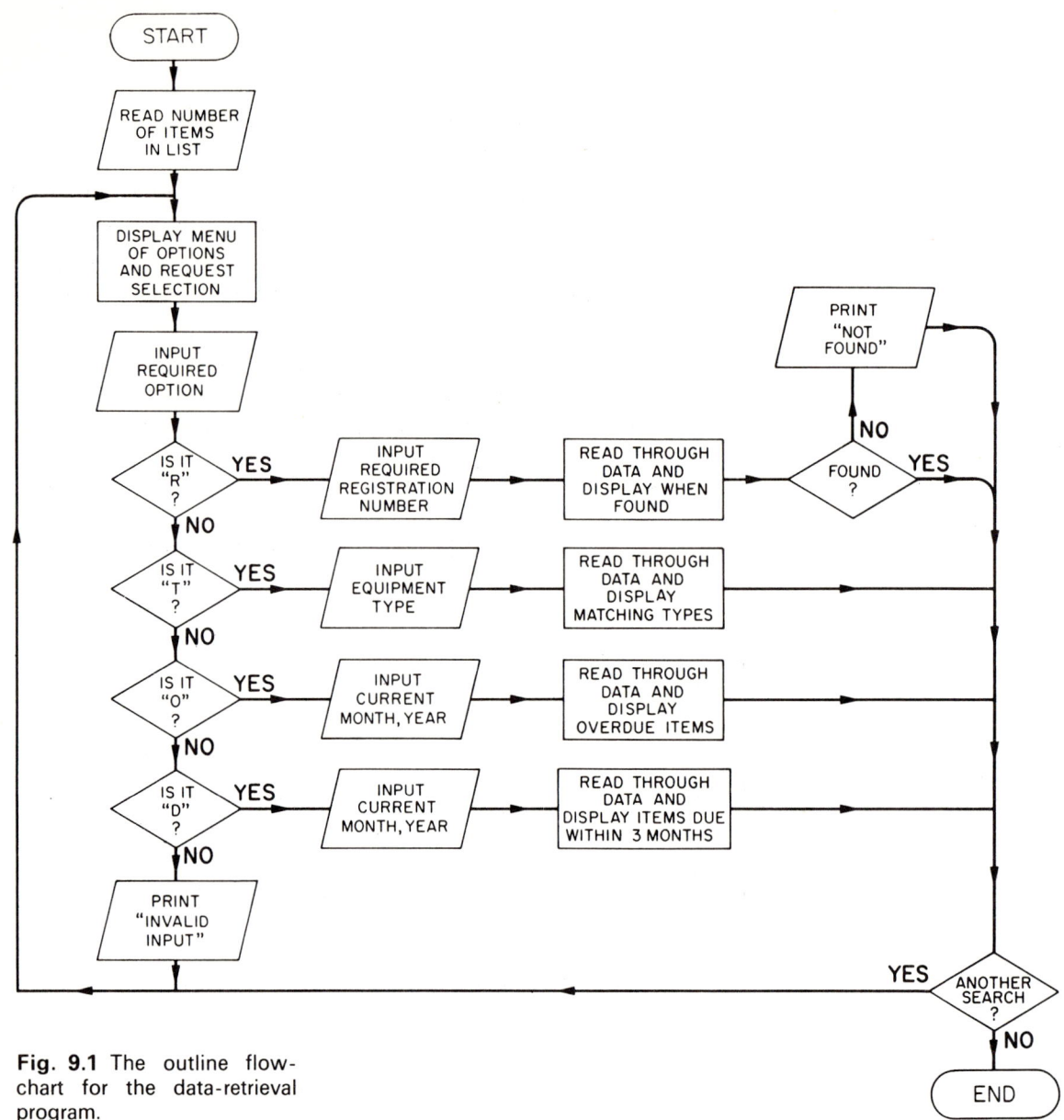

Fig. 9.1 The outline flow-chart for the data-retrieval program.

Fig. 9.2 The program listing for the data-retrieval program.

```
READY.

50 READ N
99 REM*** OPTION MENU DISPLAY
100 PRINT"DO YOU WANT TO MATCH RECORDS BY:-"
110 PRINT"                       REPLY"
120 PRINT"REGISTERED NO.      -   R"
130 PRINT"EQUIPMENT TYPE      -   T"
140 PRINT"TEST OVERDUE        -   O"
150 PRINT"DUE WITHIN 3 MONTHS -   D"
```

```
160 PRINT
170 INPUT Z$
180 IF Z$="R" THEN 300
190 IF Z$="T" THEN 400
200 IF Z$="O" THEN 500
210 IF Z$="D" THEN 600
220 PRINT"INVALID INPUT"
230 GOTO100
299 REM*** REGISTERED NO. SEARCH LOGIC
300 PRINT"INPUT REG. NO."
310 INPUT Q
320 FOR I=1 TO N
330 READ R,T$,L$,F,ML,YL
340 IF Q<>R THEN 380
350 PRINT"REG.NO.   TYPE   LOCATION FREQ. LAST TEST"
360 PRINTR;T$;L$;F;ML;YL
370 GOTO700
380 NEXT I
390 PRINT"REGISTERED NO. NOT FOUND"
395 GOTO 700
399 REM***EQUIPMENT TYPE SEARCH LOGIC"
400 PRINT"INPUT EQUIPMENT TYPE"
410 INPUT Q$
420 PRINT"REG.NO.   TYPE   LOCATION FREQ. LAST TEST"
430 FOR I=1 TO N
440 READ R,T$,L$,F,ML,YL
450 IF Q$<>T$ THEN 470
460 PRINTR;T$;L$;F;ML;YL
470 NEXT I
480 GOTO700
499 REM***TEST OVERDUE SEARCH LOGIC
500 PRINT"INPUT CURRENT MONTH NO., YEAR"
510 INPUT M,Y
520 FOR I=1 TO N
530 READR,T$,L$,F,ML,YL
535 REM*** BASED ON NO. OF MONTHS FROM JAN OF YEAR YL
540 IF (ML+F)>(M+12*(Y-YL)) THEN 560
550 PRINT"REG.NO. "R" OVERDUE FOR TEST"
560 NEXT I
570 GOTO700
599 REM***TEST DUE WITHIN 3 MONTHS SEARCH LOGIC
600 PRINT"INPUT CURRENT MONTH NO., YEAR"
610 INPUT M,Y
620 PRINT"LIST OF ITEMS REQUIRING TESTING"
621 PRINT"WITHIN THE NEXT THREE MONTHS"
629 PRINT
630 PRINT"REG.NO.   TYPE   LOCATION FREQ. LAST TEST"
640 FOR I=1 TO N
650 READ R,T$,L$,F,ML,YL
660 IF (ML+F)>(M+3+12*(Y-YL)) THEN 680
670 PRINTR;T$;L$;F;ML;YL
680 NEXT I
700 PRINT"ANOTHER SEARCH (Y OR N)"
710 INPUT Q$
720 IF Q$="N" THEN 750
730 RESTORE
740 GOTO 50
750 END
1000 DATA 6
1010 DATA 3703,COMPRESSOR,.NEW WORKS,18,3,83
1020 DATA 4129,HOIST,......NEW WORKS,12,1,83
1030 DATA 4130,PRESS,......OLD WORKS,12,5,82
1040 DATA 4206,HEATER,.....MAIN OFFICE,24,10,82
1050 DATA 5210,COMPRESSOR,.OLD WORKS,18,6,83
1060 DATA 5303,PRESS,......NEW WORKS,12,4,83
```

300–395	These deal with finding a match on a particular registered number, displaying an appropriate message if it is not found. The variables used are: R—Registered Number; T\$—Type of Equipment; L\$—Location of Equipment; F—Frequency of Testing (months); ML—Month of the Year (1–12) When Last Tested; YL—Year of Last Test (two digits).
400–480	These deal with displaying all items which are of a particular type. Note that no check is made to see if there are more matching records than would fill one screen. A counter could be included for this purpose (displaying one screen at a time until an input signal is given to move on), or printed hard-copy output could be considered.
500–570	These deal with displaying items which are overdue for testing. This condition is tested by effectively calculating when the next test is due (in months from the beginning of the year of the last test i.e. $ML+F$) and comparing it with the current month as input (on the same basis i.e. $M+12*(Y-YL)$).
600–680	These deal with displaying items which will require testing in the next three months. This is achieved by simply adding three onto the expression for the current month used above and comparing that with the calculated next test date. This method includes all overdue items in this category.
700–750	These ask if another search is required, and jump back to the start of the program if it is. Note line 730, the RESTORE statement. It is used to tell the computer to set its DATA pointer back to the first DATA statement, ready for another pass through. An alternative to this approach would have been to store the data in arrays after the first reading, but this could use up significant amounts of RAM storage.
1000–1060	These are the DATA statements. Note that lines 1010–1060 have been used with a format of one statement per item of equipment to make understanding and updating the program easier.

9.5 Demonstration runs

To illustrate the operation of the program one example of each type of match is considered below.

(a) Retrieval of a selected item by means of its registered number

In this case the option 'R' is selected from the menu, and the program requests the user to key in the registered number of the item to be retrieved, e.g. 4206. The program then reads sequentially through the DATA statements until at line 1040 it encounters data which assign the number 4206 to the variable R. When this is detected the headings and respective details for this item are displayed and the search is considered to be complete. In this case we would discover that the item is a heater located in the main office, with a two-yearly test cycle and a last inspection in October 1982. The reader may notice that the data have been arranged in ascending order of registered number. This can be useful from the point of view of easily updating the data, but it is not essential for the logic of the program which would work equally well whatever the order of the data.

(b) Retrieval of all items of a desired type

When the 'T' option is selected the program requests the user to input the character string of the type to be selected. It can be noted here that an exact match will be required, e.g. searching for a 'COMP', a 'COMPSR' or even a 'COMPRESOR' will be fruitless. This need for an exact spelling can be overcome by selecting a code letter for each type, but the consequential disadvantage is that this makes the DATA statements harder to understand. We could not simply use a first letter code for example, since HOIST and HEATER would be confused, and any other code would not be obvious without referencing a code table. Supposing that 'COMPRESSOR' was the type being searched for the program would display

REG.NO.	TYPE	LOCATION	FREQ.	LAST	TEST
3703	COMPRESSOR	.NEW WORKS	18	3	83
5210	COMPRESSOR	.OLD WORKS	18	6	83

(c) Retrieval of items whose next test is overdue

Use of option 'O' clearly requires the machine to know the current month and year, and depending on the particular type of computer being used this information can be made available in a number of ways. A mini or mainframe would probably have access to such date information without it having to be keyed in at run time, but in the case of a micro like the PET and similar machines it is simple enough to tap it in as requested. It is a matter of judgement in design as to whether this information should be requested once only at the start of the program (without knowing if it is going to be needed), whether it should be requested whenever options 'O' or 'D' are taken (which was the method adopted), or whether the more sophisticated measure of inserting a special variable is worthwhile just to detect if the information has already been input. If the current month were March 1984, then the output would be:

REG. NO. 3703 OVERDUE FOR TEST
REG. NO. 4129 OVERDUE FOR TEST
REG. NO. 4130 OVERDUE FOR TEST

(d) Retrieval of items to be tested in the next three months

Option 'D', which is perhaps the most useful way of using the program and which would probably be the justification for operating a computerised system instead of a straightforward clerical one, would give the following output if the current month were March 1984.

REG. NO.	TYPE	LOCATION	FREQ.	LAST	TEST
3703	COMPRESSOR.	NEW WORKS	18	3	83
4129	HOIST.....	NEW WORKS	12	1	83
4130	PRESS.....	OLD WORKS	12	5	82
5303	PRESS.....	NEW WORKS	12	4	83

9.6 Similar applications

As an indication of the wide range of applications that programs of this sort can be used for, consider the following examples.

(i) Personnel training records. Individual's names, job titles, locations and information on courses attended (with dates) would be on file. Options to select everyone who has attended a particular course or everyone who has not attended a course for a particular length of time, as well as the more obvious selection by name, could be on the 'menu'.

(ii) Drawing records. The reference numbers of drawings, the date when they were done, the buildings, items of equipment, or plant depicted etc. would be the information on file. Options to select by reference number and see displayed a description of what the drawing contains, or to select an item which may be contained in several drawings and see displayed the reference numbers of the relevant drawings, could all be on the 'menu'.

(iii) Good pub guide. The name, location and brewery, would be

on file together with information on the food and games facilities etc. The 'menu' could include options to select by name, or to select all pubs in a particular locality, or all pubs belonging to a particular brewery, or a combination of these factors such as locality, food and games. The method of dealing with selection against several criteria at once is to use IF statements with more than one comparison in them. For example,

```
1000   IF T$ = "WARRINGTON"  AND  B$ = "GREENALLS"
       THEN 2000
```

Finally it is worth restating that the formulation of this program for information retrieval was used to illustrate the programming principles involved, and that for large volumes of data with frequent updating, the use of disk or tape files would be more appropriate.

Exercises 9

1 Modify the registered-number search of the program listed in this chapter so as to include a display of the date (month, year) in which the next test is due.
2 Modify the overdue-for-test search of the program to print an appropriate message if there are no overdue items.
3 Identify an application of a retrieval program, of the type described in this chapter, based on your own experience. It may be serious or not but you should identify exactly what data items would be required and what search options should be provided.
4 Create some test data for your application and write down what results you would expect from some typical uses of the search options.
5 Write and test your program.
6 Explain the factors that influence the design of an information retrieval program.

10 Systems Analysis

10.1 Introduction

Systems analysis is the design of programs to control and monitor the way in which the computer performs its tasks. This function is described in some detail in the first part of this chapter and briefly covers the activities necessary to design and set up a computer system. The second part of the chapter is devoted to section A of the syllabus of the TEC Computer Assignments (level II) unit (U80/720), which requires the student to be able to analyse an existing computer system as a case study. This can be achieved most effectively through an understanding of the processes and problems that had to be tackled by the original systems analyst. The stages in systems analysis can be categorised as follows, each category being described in full in the next few pages.

(i) Feasibility study.
(ii) Systems report.
(iii) Program specification.
(iv) Implementation.
(v) Systems appraisal.

10.2 The feasibility study

Before any large investment of time or money is made to a new project, it is common sense to make sure, as far as is reasonably possible, that the techniques the system uses will be able to do the job, that the likely costs are acceptable, and that using a computer is really the best way to do the job. This process is referred to as a feasibility study. The first requirement is a clearly stated terms of reference document, in which the people who are going to pay for the system describe what they want the system to achieve. This is the first hurdle because the potential user of the system is not usually familiar with the precise capabilities of the computer, so that the systems analyst has the task of translating what is required into a statement which defines the scope of the new system, within the limitations of the technology to hand. In this situation there is plenty of scope for the original intentions of the user to be misunderstood or misrepresented, and for both parties to be unaware of their subtly different viewpoints. Any student analysing an existing system is strongly recommended to investigate the early history of that system, to learn from the lessons it contains.

The estimate of cost must include the cost of the initial study, the computer hardware that will be committed to the application, and the operating cost in terms of manpower and materials. The estimate of benefits should be made after a consideration of the human factors involved, and potential problems arising from any changes in staff operating practice should be clearly set out. This stage is concluded when the results of the study have been discussed with the client, and when a written directive for the future of the project is given to the systems analyst.

10.3 The systems report

At this stage the work begins in earnest, for the systems analyst will need to find out, in full detail, exactly which items of data are to be the input for the new system, what the rules are which will determine how they are to be manipulated or processed, and which items are to be the output and in what format they are required. Having established these facts the analyst will then need to draw on his creative talents to devise an efficient system to meet their needs. A cornerstone of his design will be the logical structure of the files of information that the system will process. The factors to be considered here are whether the files should be of a sequential nature, with logical records being processed one after another in a specified sequence of key fields (e.g. ascending sequence of invoice number or employee number); or whether they should be of a direct-access type allowing random selection of any record as and when required. The type of file structure will influence the storage media (direct access being restricted to appropriate devices), and so will file sizes and retrieval-speed requirements.

The report will contain a systems diagram, showing the logical stages of the data processing and the flow of data from input to output, in particular indicating which files and operations are used at each stage. The form of this diagram will depend on the standards of the computing organisation. They range from the highly pictorial diagram of Figure 1.1 or diagrams using symbols to represent hardware as in Section 10.7(d), to, at the other extreme, structured analysis methods in which the flow of data is represented using symbols without assuming anything about the computer hardware to be used.

The report will also contain examples of any documents or screen layouts that will be used to capture data, as well as examples of output report and screen formats. A refined statement of costs and benefits will be included in the report, and it will form the basis on which the clients will be asked to make a firm written commitment for the system to go ahead.

10.4 Program specification

At this stage the analyst will break down the processing requirements into manageable chunks, for each of which he will specify the detailed requirements to be achieved by a computer program. This will be written by a programmer. A feature of this stage will be the planning of tests and test data, both to be used by the programmer and to enable the system to be thoroughly tested.

10.5 Implementation

Before the system can 'go live', the people who are going to use it must be trained in the new procedures, and user guides to the system should be produced for their reference. A period of 'parallel running' may be appropriate if the system is a large one, and this involves operating old and new systems side by side as a way of checking that the new system is acceptable before abandoning the old.

10.6 Systems appraisal

This stage covers the entire post-implementation history of a system. It should include a definite 'taking stock' session in which everyone's views on the project are heard. There should at least be a recognised channel through which feedback on desirable modifications can be made known to the analyst, so that changes can be made at appropriate stages as the system evolves (always provided that the effort involved is worthwhile). Any analysis of an existing system should include discussions with some of the people who use it, because their views will often shed new light on the bare bones of the computer technology.

10.7 Analysing a case study

To illustrate the things to look out for in analysing a case study this section considers an imaginary stock-control system in a medium sized business. The main feature of the system is that it automatically re-orders a set quantity of a stock item whenever its stock level falls below a set re-order level.

(a) The problem being solved

A first stage in the analysis will be the definition of the problem that the computer system is solving. Drawing a comparison with the original analyst's role, it would be useful to see the original terms of reference and to consider whether the system meets their requirements in its current form. It should be possible at this stage to identify the benefits that the computer system was designed to achieve. For example in our stock-control system, the basic problem might have been a manual system which required a lot of clerical effort, but which lacked real control over stocks, and which did not enable the stock situation to be easily assessed from locations far away from the stores. The benefits of the computer system would then be reduced clerical effort, an economic level of stocks, a better availability of stock items, and more readily accessible information on current stock levels.

(b) Input data, output data and files

A computer system which tackles a real life problem will be a complex affair with different programs being used at appropriate times. The analysis of inputs and outputs will therefore need to be carried out separately with reference to each stage in the operation of the system. To understand the structure of the system it is a good idea to examine the central file or files around which the system is based. For example in our case study we may have a file composed of records with the fields shown in Table 10.1. The unused field is useful should any extra information require to be included in the system as it evolves, and it also brings the record length to a total of 128 characters, which is often a convenient size to include an exact number of records in one block of the storage medium. It is important to consider why the particular method of storage has been chosen: in our case

Table 10.1

Field number	Field name	Field length	Field type
1	Item code	6	numbers
2	Item description	20	letters
3	Item purchase price	8	numbers
4	Current stock level	6	numbers
5	Re-order level	6	numbers
6	Re-order quantity	6	numbers
7	Delivery lead time (days)	3	numbers
8	Date of last order	6	numbers
9	Outstanding order indicator	1	letter
10	Supplier codes	3 × 8	numbers
11	Unused field	42	—

study for example a magnetic disk with a random-access file structure is likely to be used because the types of processing (interrogation for particular stock items) will require fast system-response times. Inputs and outputs will be related to the following programs.

Record creation/amendment. This program will certainly be required to correct any discrepancies between actual stock details and the computer records, and it will be used to create new records. Input may therefore consist of any or all of fields 1–10, and output will be fields 1–11. (It is common practice to rewrite entire blocks of disk data when even minor changes are made to fields of one record in the block.) This program may well be used to update stock levels and reset the outstanding order indicator when deliveries are made against an external order from a supplier.

Stock-status enquiry. This program will enable the current data for a particular item code to be displayed, most likely by means of an on-line visual display unit. Input is therefore an item code and output may again be any subset or all of fields 1–10. For stock taking etc. a full file printout will be an option.

Stock-requisition request. This program will allow the originator, subject to certain password-type security checks, to initiate on demand the printing of a stock requisition in the stores. The input of the program will therefore include a security code, the identity of the originating department, item codes and item quantities. Some supplier preference may also be indicated here. Output will be a printed requisition and a screen acknowledgement or warning message (if for example the quantity required exceeds the current stock level). If the stock of the desired item falls below the re-order level as a result of this current requisition, then an output entry should be made in the external order file, and the outstanding order indicator should be set to 'Y' as well as the date of last order being set to the current date on the item's main file record.

Daily external-order program. This program, run daily perhaps at around 3 p.m., will take as input the external order file produced by the last program and a supplier name and address file so that the external orders may be printed as hard-copy output.

Weekly order progress chasing. On a weekly basis this program will be run to print a report of all items which have outstanding external orders with an elapsed time since ordering in excess of 25% over the normal delivery lead time. (Clearly this criterion will depend on the type of business concerned, and in particular for items with very long lead times a fixed number of days overdue may be used instead.) Input here is the main item-details file, and output will be the printed list of orders to be chased. It is assumed that the current date is available to all programs as a part of the system.

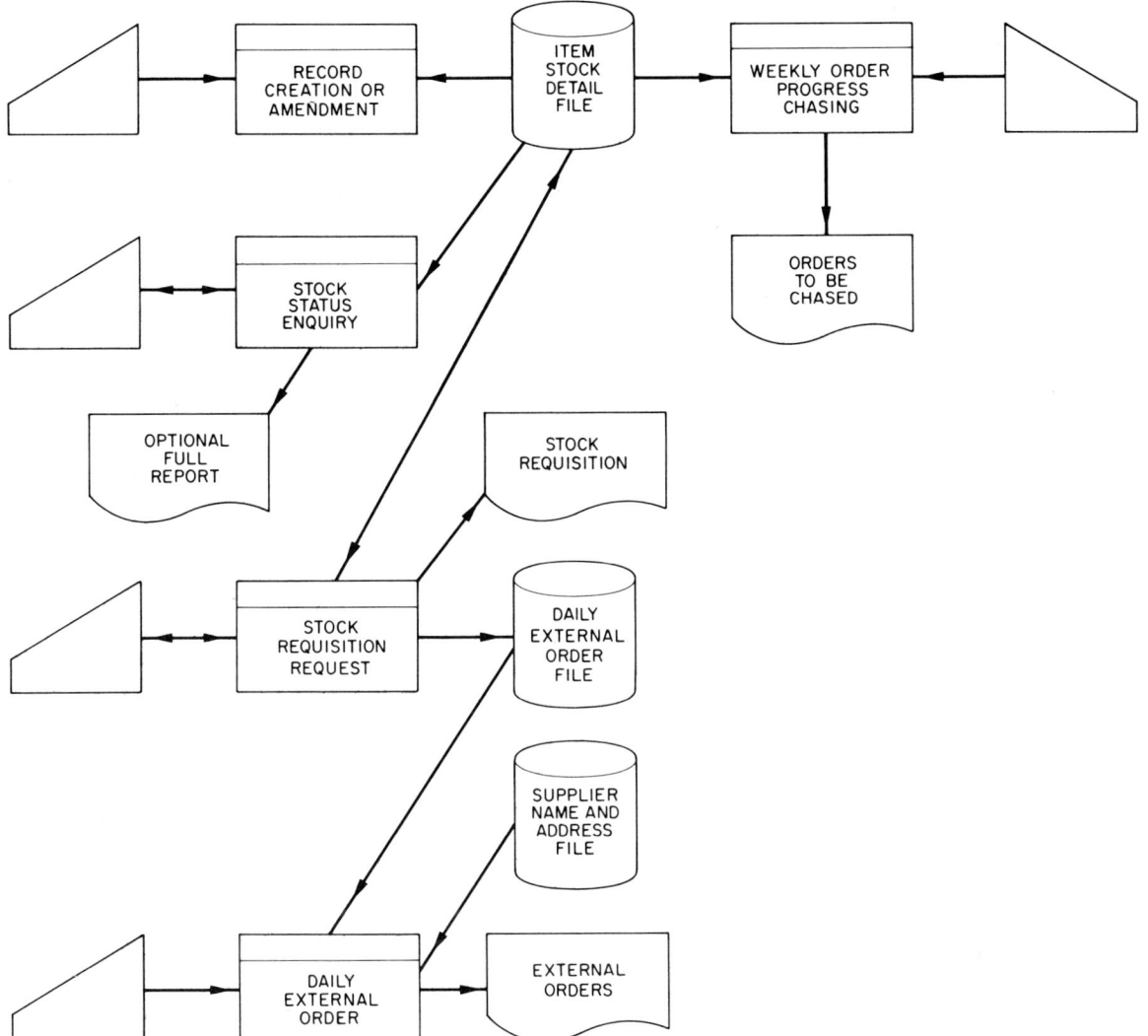

Fig. 10.1 The flowchart for a stock-control system.

(c) The system flowchart

Figure 10.1 is a system flowchart illustrating the suite of programs which make up the computer system and showing their input and output files. (In this context a stream of keyboard data or a printed tabulation are regarded as files.)

The symbols used in system flowcharts such as Figure 10.1 are not as universally standardised as those adopted for program flowcharts, but a suggested scheme is given in Table 10.2.

Whatever the choice of symbols to be used, the important function of a system flowchart is to demonstrate the input/output files and media to be employed in making the system work, and to give an impression of the logical sequence of operations. Finally,

Table 10.2

Symbol	Description
#L 507 / ORDER ENTRY	A major program with identification number (for operating purposes in the top section.
ORDERS (disk)	A magnetic-disk file (hard disk).
VEHICLE DETAILS (floppy)	A magnetic-disk file (floppy disk).
EMPLOYEE TAX CODES (tape)	A magnetic-tape file.
TABULATION	Printed hard-copy output.
(trapezoid)	A VDU or teletype terminal with a keyboard entry.
→	A flowline indicating the direction of data flow.
(lightning bolt)	A data flow which makes use of a telecommunications link.

since the purpose of the flowchart is to communicate, and since attention must be attracted for this to happen, it is worth considering the use of some 'once-off' symbols (such as the telephone and the truck of Figure 1.1) in order to add interest!

(d) Evaluating a system

The first criteria in evaluating a system are the two questions, 'Does it work?', and, 'Is it being used?'. It is an indictment of the computing profession that the answers to these questions are not always an unequivocal, 'Yes'. To qualify these two bald questions it is necessary to compare what the system is achieving with the intended aims of the original terms of reference, and to assess whether the predicted benefits of the system have been realised in practice. As far as our case study is concerned for example:

- Can the current stock levels of items be displayed within an acceptable response time?
- Do the users of the system have confidence in the figures being displayed?
- Has anyone calculated the savings actually achieved through reduced stockholdings?
- Have late deliveries from suppliers been chased up more effectively?
- Has the frequency with which stocks have run out been acceptable?
- Have the forecast savings in clerical effort been translated into real benefits?

At a more general level the following points are worth considering.

- Has the system made appropriate use of the technology? (Look out for situations where the hardware is excessive for the task in hand, is used inefficiently or, alternatively, where a machine and storage are hopelessly overloaded.)
- Does the system offer a growth path (i.e. a clear route for the development of hardware and software) as the application matures?
- Has sufficient notice been taken of feedback from the users, and has the system been modified as a result? (Note however that the need for excessive modification is a worse crime than poor follow-up support!)

As a final word on evaluation consult the users for their feelings about the computer system, but be sure to get representative views from each area that the system affects, since an improvement in one department's operations may be at the expense of dissatisfaction elsewhere, and the important factor is the total impact on the business.

(e) Reporting your analysis

A report describing the analysis and evaluation of a case study should have a clearly defined structure, so that the various observations can be assimilated easily. One suggestion for a structure is given below.

- Introduction. This describes the terms of reference for the original system and setting the background to the application.
- Data description. This defines the inputs, outputs and data files used in the system, with comments on the media used to store the information.
- System description. This includes a system flowchart with supporting text describing how the system is operated.
- Evaluation. This is an assessment of the effectiveness of the computer system with some evidence of probing beneath the superficial system's documentation.

A great benefit of analysis and evaluation is the identification of good points to build on, and bad points to avoid, leading to better systems in the future. A carefully written report of this nature can therefore be a very valuable document.

Exercises 10

1. List the major steps in the systems analysis for a computer application and describe one of them in detail.
2. Draw a system flowchart for a computer system that you are familiar with, and list the contents of the data files that are used.
3. Discuss the factors that would affect the choice of media for, and organisation of, the storage of data in the design of a computer system.
4. Describe the design of a computer system for monitoring the progress of work being done in an engineering workshop, making assumptions about the volumes of data to be handled (say what these are) and the level of sophistication required. The design should include:
- fast retrieval of the current status of any piece of work (e.g. queuing, finished, partly done);
- regular reports of work done in the workshop in a given period;
- a scheduling program to allocate a start time, and the resources required, for all work awaiting attention (details of the scheduling algorithm should be ignored);
- automatic logging of charges to the department or customer for whom the work is being done.
5. Describe the data files to be used in question 4.
6. Draw a system flowchart for the system of question 4.

Appendix: Suggestions for Program Assignments

A1.1 Overview

Searching for inspiration for a computer program assignment to meet the requirements of a syllabus such as that of the BTEC Computer Assignments unit can be a difficult task. The root of the difficulty lies not with the student's ability, but rather in the process of identifying which project to attempt. The key factor is that any project that is chosen should appeal to the student as being of intrinsic interest, or of direct relevance to a real-life problem with which he is associated. This interest is necessary to sustain the hard work required to turn ideas into well documented programs. This appendix is offered as a source for generating ideas that the students themselves should develop with a sense of ownership.

A1.2 Categories

Program assignments can be very roughly categorised as follows.

(a) Calculations

(i) Formulae. Formulae may be used to carry out conversions as in our Centigrade to Fahrenheit example, or iterative approximations as in Newton's Method. Here the programs are characterised by the small volume of data input and output.

(ii) Analyses. Analyses or summaries use relatively large quantities of input data which are processed to arrive at a small but meaningful set of results, as for example in the statistical analysis of questionnaire replies, exam results, or technical observations. The statistical theory need not be more sophisticated than the calculation of an average value and the identification of maximum and minimum observations. Here we have a high volume of data input and small output requirements.

(iii) Displays, tabulations and simulations. Graphic displays, tabulations of mathematical functions for a range of values, and simulations of real situations all use a relatively small amount of input data to generate a large amount of output. A simple

simulation could model the arrival and queueing of jobs to be processed by a particular machine, with the job duration being randomly determined.

(b) Data file manipulations

(i) Information retrieval. Information retrieval involves the use of certain key fields to retrieve particular records, or to enable selection of records to be made against certain criteria (see Chapter 9).

(ii) File Processing. File processing is a more difficult type of programming to accommodate at this level because of the practical complications of file housekeeping. It involves the use of arithmetic rules, which are usually simple, to process one or more files of input data. An example would be the processing of a file of individual sales transactions together with a file of customer details, to produce a composite tabulation with customer details and summarised sales to that customer.

(c) Recreations

These cover much the same area as calculations but with the subtle difference that the application has a competitive or humorous interest, or maybe in the case of an animated-graphics display is simply fascinating to watch.

A1.3 Examples

This section gives examples in each of the above categories, with some hints and useful approaches, but in the author's experience there is no better motivating factor than a student's desire to see his own version of an idea in action.

(a) Calculations

(i) Formulae. Examples include linear conversions, areas and volumes.

1 The volume of a spherical cap of height h from a sphere of radius R is calculated using the formula

$$V = \frac{1}{3}\pi h^2 (3R - h)$$

2 Particle dynamics use the formulae

$$v = u + ft$$
$$v^2 = u^2 + 2fs$$
$$s = ut + \tfrac{1}{2}ft^2$$

where u = initial velocity
v = new velocity
t = elapsed time
f = acceleration   (deceleration is conventionally negative)
s = distance travelled

3   Projectile trajectories (initial velocity V fired at angle A to the horizontal) use

$$\text{horizontal range} = \frac{V^2}{g} \sin 2A$$

$$\text{highest point} = \frac{V^2 \sin^2 A}{2g}$$

$$\text{time of flight} = \frac{2V}{g} \sin A \qquad (g = 980.62 \text{ cm s}^{-2})$$

4   Formulae for the evaluation of powers, roots or mathematical expressions (e.g. sums of series) may also be used.

(ii) Analyses.
1   The arithmetic mean and standard deviation of a set of observations or samples may be calculated.
2   Try the ranking of marks into order of merit (together with the names of the scorers) or the preparation of league tables to rank and record performances in sports or competitions. A similar table of accident avoidance at work would be possible.
3   Summarise experimental observations in histogram or frequency distribution form.

(iii) Displays, tabulations and simulations.
1   Evaluate powers, roots or mathematical expressions for a range of values in tabular form.
2   Expand a series of numbers from some generating rule such as
$$N(I) = N(I-1) + N(I-2).$$
3   Try plotting histograms or graphs.
4   Calculate values of time dependent variables over a given time interval.
5   Produce a graphic display of the above variables, e.g. stock-tank levels or space-craft positions (see question 5 of Exercises 5). The basic concept of animation is that to give the impression of movement the picture for a particular instant must have the moving parts blanked out (with the space bar character for example) and then displayed in another part of the screen to which they will appear to have moved.
6   For intensity or contour plots print a symbol in each position on a graph corresponding to the value of some expression at that point. The basic technique is to use a character string, say of 5 characters, such as A$ =" . + * ■ " and then derive an integer from 1 to 5 from the expression as for example in

$$I = 5*(X*Y/5 - INT(X*Y/5)) + 1$$

for the expression X∗Y, and finally to display MID$(A$,I,1) which will be a character whose intensity reflects the value of the expression at that point.

(b) Data file manipulations

(i) Information retrieval.
1   Equipment reliability records list type of equipment, registration number, location and number of breakdowns, retrieve by type, registration number, location or number of breakdowns where they are in excess of some specified figure.
2   Personnel records, show the name, identification number, job title, department, location, telephone number, home address and qualifications and skills of employees. These allow retrieval of specified individuals' records or selection by qualifications or skills.
3   A good pub guide would include details of brewery, location, facilities and special attractions; for retrieval of details of specific pubs or selection of a list of pubs satisfying certain criteria.

(ii) File processing.
1   Updating cumulative sales, usage or breakdown data might be done using a daily file to update a weekly summary file which may be used in turn to update a monthly file (showing cumulative figures for the year to date, maybe even with last year's figures for comparison). Such suites of programs can easily require major analysis and programming effort, and should not be attempted unless the student is carrying out such a project for an employer and has some professional help available.

(c) Recreations

1   Try simple quizzes, code guessing games of the 'Mastermind' type, hangman (with or without graphics), and battleships.
2   Target games, in which an animated display is used to fire a missile at a moving target, are popular. The definitive (but far too ambitious) example is 'Space Invaders'.
3   Graphic displays can be created by random or mathematical procedures, with or without animation. These can be fascinating to just sit and watch, and can range from an identikit-type build up of cartoon faces, to illustrations of simple machines in action.
4   Types of computer generated text·vary from the selection of the contents of a document from many possible constituent standard paragraphs, to computer poetry (randomly selecting words from groups of nouns, adjectives, adverbs, verbs and prepositions). Phrase structures can be selected at random from a set of possible word-type combinations.

Index

ABS function, 52
absolute value, 52, 67
access time, 20
ALGOL, 29
analogue computers, 1
analogue to digital conversion, 26
AND condition, 43
animation, 105
applications, 2–4
    packages, 9, 27
    programmers, 7
arrays
    numeric, 57
    string, 57–8
arithmetic
    priorities, 36–7
    unit, 15
assembly-level languages, 29
assignments, 103–6

back-up, 32
BASIC, 29, 39–63
batch processing, 3
binary digits, 15, 30
bit-image processing, 26
block
    disk, 18, 31, 97
    magnetic-tape, 21
brackets, in BASIC, 37
bubble sort, 70–2
byte, 18

calculation
    package, 32–4
    assignments, 103–4
card reader, 24
case studies, 4–12, 96–102
cash flow example, 33
cassette drives, 21
chain printer, 24
clear screen key, 63, 79
COBOL, 29
comment statements, 73
commercial data-processing, 3, 4–12
compilation, 29–30
compiler, 30
concatenation, 50

contour plot, 105–6
control devices, 25–6
control unit, 16
COS function, 54, 82–3
cursor addressing, 62–3, 78–9, 84
cylinder, magnetic disk, 19

daisy-wheel print-head, 23
data
    entry, 24
    fields, 32, 97
    retrieval, 86–93
DATA statement, 58–9, 86–92
decision flowchart symbol, 66
digital
    computers, 1–2
    computing, 2–4
DIMENSION statement, 58
direct access, 20, 95
distributed processing, 3
drawing records application, 92
documentation, 65, 72–5
double-density disks, 18
dummy argument, 52

effluent control, 25
electrical equipment example, 31
END statement, 46
execution, 29–30
exponentiation, 36

feasibility study, 94–5
file
    accumulation and summary, 12
    display and search, 11–12
    management package, 31–2
    processing, 104, 106
firmware, 16
floppy disks, 17–19
flowcharts
    program, 65–72
    system, 99–100
flowline, 66
FOR. . . . NEXT instruction, 41–2
FORTRAN, 29

GET statement, 61

golf-ball print-head, 23
good pub guide application, 92–3, 106
GOSUB statement, 59–60
GOTO statement, 42–3
graph program, 76–85
growth path, 101

hard-copy, 32, 73
hard disks, 19
hardware, 9, 14–26
high-level languages, 29
home cursor key, 63, 79, 84
housekeeping, resource, 22
hybrid computers, 1

IF statement, 43–4
    with string variable, 48
implementation, 96
information retrieval, 104, 106
ink-jet printer, 24
input devices, 15
INPUT statement, 38–40
input/output devices, 17–26
INT function, 51–2
interactive computing, 4
interpreters, 30
iterative methods
    example, 46–7
    flowchart, 67–8

jump, 42

K, 18
key-to-disk systems, 24

laser printer, 24
latency time, 20
LEN string function, 50–1
LET statement, 40–1
line numbers, 37, 81
liveware, 7
LOAD command, 62
LOG function, 54
loop, 41
loop variable, 42
low-level language, 29

Index

machine code, 30
magnetic-disk drives, 17–21
magnetic-tape drives, 21–2
mainframe, 2
matrix print-head, 23
megabyte, 19
memory, 15
menu, 89
microcomputer, 2
   applications, 10–12
microprocessors, 2, 15
MID$ string function, 49–50
minicomputer, 2
   applications, 8–10
mini-floppy disk, 17
mnemonic codes, 27, 29
modulus, 67
multi-programming, 28
multi-task processing, 4

NEXT statement, 41–2
NEW command, 62
Newton's method
   example, 46–7
   flowchart, 67–8
null string, 61
number crunching, 3
numerical analysis, 8

object program, 30
office of the future, 12
off-line processing, 4
off-page connector, 66
on-line processing, 4
operating system, 16, 28
operators, computer, 7
OR condition, 43
order/invoice example, 5–7
output devices, 15

package, software, 28, 30–4
paper-tape reader, 24
parabola, 81
parallel running, 96
personnel training records example, 92
pi, 83
PL/1, 29
plotting program, 76–85
pools forecast program, 52–3
PRINT statement, 37–8
printers
   line, 24
   serial, 23–4
processing, 3–4

program, 27, 37
   specification, 72–3, 96
programmers
   applications, 7
   systems, 8
programming language, 27, 28–9

quadratic equation flowchart, 68–9

radian measure, 83
RAM, 15
random access, 20
random number generation, 52–3
READ statement, 58–9
read/write
   heads, 19
   window, 18
real time, 3
recreational applications, 3, 104, 106
REMARK statement, 51, 73
renumbering lines, 81
repeated fields, 32
resolution, 76, 78, 82
RESTORE statement, 59, 90
return key, 38
RETURN statement, 59–60
reverse field, 80
RND function, 52–3
ROM, 15, 16
rounding, 51–2
RUN command, 37, 62
RVS key, 80

SAVE command, 62
scientific applications, 8
seek time, 19
sector, 18, 31
sensing devices, 25
sequential
   access, 21, 95
   processing, 22
simulation, 8, 29, 52, 61, 103–4
SIN function, 54
software, 9, 27–8
sort, 70–2
source program, 30
spreadsheet package, 32–4, 60
SQR function, 54
stock control case study, 96–102
STR$ string function, 50
string
   functions, 49
   length, 50–1

string (contd.)
   variables, 48
structure of a computer, 14–16
subroutines, 59–61
symbols
   program flowchart, 66
   system flowchart, 100
syntax, 30
system commands, 62
systems
   analysts, 8
   appraisal, 96
   diagram, 95
   evaluation, 102
   programmers, 8
   report, 95–6, 101–2

TAB function, 54, 80
technical applications, 8
terminal program flowchart symbol, 66
terms of reference, 94, 97
test data, 75, 81–5, 96
text strings, 48
time series, 44
time sharing, 4
track, 18
transfer time, 20
trigonometric functions, 54
truncation, 51
types
   of computer, 1
   of computing, 2–4

user guide, 73, 96
utility programs, 27

VAL string function, 50
validity checking, 6, 32, 61, 89
variable
   array, 57
   initialisation, 42
   list, 74
   numeric, 38–40
   string, 48
VDU, 22–3
visual display unit, 22–3
voice input, 26

Winchester technology disks, 19
word processors, 12
workstation, 12
write protect tabs, 18–19